A Childhood IN THE Australian Bush

Dr Kerry Breen AO is a retired physician whose career spanned roles in clinical medicine, medical education, medical ethics, regulation of the medical profession and the health of doctors. In retirement he has pursued a deep interest in writing. His two most recent books are *A Perilous Profession: The Dangerous Lives of Doctors* and *Wrongful Convictions in Australia: Addressing Issues in the Criminal Justice System* (the latter with Dr Stephen Cordner).

By the Author—

A Perilous Profession: The Dangerous Lives of Doctors, 2023

Wrongful Convictions in Australia: Addressing Issues in the Criminal Justice System, 2023

Good Medical Practice: Professionalism, Ethics and Law, 2016

Memoir of an accidental ethicist: On medical ethics, medical misconduct and challenges for the medical profession, 2018

A Passion for Justice: The Life and Times of Forensic Pathologist, Vernon Plueckhahn, 2019

The Man We Never Knew: Carl de Gruchy, Medical Pioneer, 2019

So You Want To Be a Doctor: A Guide For Prospective and Current Medical Students in Australia, 2020

Humanity in Medicine: The Life of Physician Dr Stanley Goulston, 2020

Ten Thousand Heart Operations: The Life of Cardio-Thoracic Surgeon Dr John Clarebrough, 2022

A Childhood IN THE Australian Bush

KERRY BREEN

ARCADIA

First published 2024 by Arcadia
the general books' imprint of
Australian Scholarly Publishing
7 Lt Lothian St North
North Melbourne, Vic 3051
tel: 61 3 93296963
contact@scholarly.info / www.scholarly.com

ISBN 978-1-923068-95-7

Cover Design: Daniel Strojek
Cover Image: Provided by Kerry Breen

Contents

Prologue

The 'bush' has a particular meaning for Australians. It has some similarity with the Australian term 'outback' although the latter implies more remoteness from our coastline and our cities. The 'bush' signifies a strong distinction from urban living and a sense of living in a remote rural community. To my mind the term implies also a sense of distance from the amenities of urban living, a sense of isolation, and a sense of needing to be able to cope with aspects of daily life that most Australians nowadays cannot imagine. It may be best encapsulated in the term 'bush school'.

This memoir describes a childhood spent in remote parts of north-eastern Victoria in the 1940s and 50s. My family moved to live in that region because my father was a primary school teacher. The first two primary schools in which I was taught by my father were in tiny settlements with very small populations. Both schools closed long ago. My story not only covers my experience of a childhood in the bush but also is a record of the challenges that bush school teachers faced in that era. My father taught in eight Victorian bush schools from 1929 until 1955.

Towards the end of his life at which time he was a widower living alone at Rye, a beachside town on the Mornington Peninsula, my father began writing his own memoir. Sadly his health faded and his memoir was not completed. We found it amongst his possessions after his death. It was hand-written but easily deciphered. His style of writing is unusual but very entertaining. It is also informative in regard to the training and work experiences of primary school teachers in the first half of the last century. I have attached it as an appendix to my own memoir.

I

Arrival at Freeburgh

In January 1941, my father*, a primary school teacher, arrived in Freeburgh in north-eastern Victoria with my mother† and my two older siblings, Michael aged six and Jennifer aged four years. My father had been appointed as the head master (and only teacher) to the Freeburg Primary School (No 895). I was not yet born as my birth took place at the nearby Bright Bush Nursing Hospital later that same year.

Freeburgh was then a very small town. Situated in the Ovens Valley six miles (ten kilometres) south of the larger town of Bright, it barely deserved the description of a town. It consisted essentially of the single room primary school, the adjacent teacher's residence, and the Freeburgh community hall situated nearby but on the other side of the only road in the valley. The road was known then as the Ovens Valley Highway but is now part of the 'Great Alpine Way'. The Ovens Valley Highway led south to Harrietville and Mt Hotham and north to Wangaratta. Half a mile down the valley from the school lived our nearest neighbours, the Flynn family. They ran the local Post Office from a front room of their home. There were four or five other homes dispersed around the district, all on small farms, with one farm also hosting an apple orchard. There were no shops, no hotels, and no

---

* Baptised Michael Leo, my father as an adult was known as Leo Breen.
† Ellen Mary Breen (née Zeven) was always known as Molly.

churches at Freeburgh. The district was scattered with evidence of the activities of past settlers in the form of imported chestnut trees, walnut trees and blackberry bushes, now growing mostly on public land.

My father's move followed a three-year stint as headmaster and only teacher at Ocean Grove, which is south of Geelong and was then only a tiny hamlet. That school had an enrolment of around 25 pupils. As my father was a teacher with over ten years of experience, the move to remote Freeburgh seems surprising. It did not reflect well on his teaching abilities or his love of teaching. In applying for this posting, he later stated that he was influenced by his desire to find a school that came with a teacher's residence. That he ended up so far away from his and his wife's families in Melbourne may also have had some relationship with the outbreak of World War II but equally might have been connected to the uncomfortable relationship he had with the bureaucrats in the Education Department and its employees, and especially his intense dislike of school inspectors, all former teachers.

The school teacher's residence at Freeburgh circa 1941
(Michael and Jennifer were probably waiting for a swim in the Ovens River)

As an appendix to this book you will find my father's unpublished incomplete account of his early life and training to become a teacher. He wrote this autobiography by hand towards the end of his life. Sadly, illness prevented him from completing it. After he died in 1983, we found it among his possessions. He wrote legibly so typing it for publication was straightforward. I have added a few explanatory notes to the typed version. This account explains when and how his dislike of school inspectors arose. It also describes the pathway into school-teaching a century ago. My father wrote poetry, much of which was published. He identifies a couple of these poems in his story.

If there are readers who have not heard of Freeburgh, I will be unsurprised. There are a large number of small towns in Victoria of which I have never heard. Some that I do know of are places where my father taught school before I was born. These included the tiny towns of Arawata in Gippsland, and Lubeck and Coromby in the Wimmera.

Before the start of the 20th century, Freeburgh was a thriving community. In the early 1800s the Ovens Valley was settled by farmers who followed the Ovens River south from Wangaratta as there was fertile soil in the valley. Those early settlers observed the seasonal movement of Aboriginal people to Mt Bogong for their annual feasting on the large moths that we now call the Bogong moth. By 1941, sadly I doubt that there were any Aboriginal people remaining in the Ovens Valley.

The development of Freeburgh as a township was based on the Victorian gold rush which began at Ballarat in 1851. In 1852 gold was discovered at Beechworth and in 1853 gold was also discovered at Buckland in the Ovens Valley not far from Freeburgh. Prospectors flocked in from all over the world. They sought alluvial gold from the Ovens River and Morse's Creek which joins the Ovens River at a site that became the township of Bright. They also dug mine shafts in the foothills on the sides of the valley. In the early 1900s, investors poured money into gold-dredging in the Ovens Valley and it was said that by 1910 there were forty dredges in the area.

Some of the early prospectors came from Germany. Freeburgh is assumed to be named after Freiburg in Germany. This seems likely as Freiburg is near the Black Forest and is surrounded by heavily wooded hills; a homesick German may have seen some similarity in the landscape. As further evidence of German prospectors, a little closer to Bright there is a former settlement that was given the name of Germantown.

A school was first opened at Freeburgh in 1865 but the school building in which my father taught was constructed in 1916. At around 1900, the school at Freeburgh accommodated up to 100 pupils. By the time that my father arrived in 1941, the enrolment had dropped to around twenty pupils and those numbers gradually declined while we lived there.

The Freeburg Primary School (No 895) circa 1925. The teacher's residence is in the background

In the 1880's, at the height of development from the gold rush, in addition to a school and a post office, Freeburgh boasted two hotels, a public library and a sawmill. None of these latter buildings were evident in 1941. The population in the 1881 census was 269 people but by the 1933 census the population had fallen to 88. In 1941, my estimate of the population in the district was around 30 to 40 people, including children.

Although the 'town' of Freeburgh was dying in the 1940s, near-by Bright was flourishing. The Victorian Railways had helped it to become a tourist destination as a railway spur had been built from the main line at Wangaratta, initially to Myrtleford, and extended to Bright in 1890. The availability of travel by train from Melbourne via Wangaratta also helped the early popularity of the large chalet on top of nearby Mt Buffalo which opened in 1910.

As a young boy at Freeburgh, I cannot recall it ever snowing in the floor of the Ovens Valley. In winter we could see the snow-covered peak of Mt Feathertop when we stood on the road outside the school grounds. The Australian Alps are to some extent a misnomer as the mountains are not especially high and as the tops of several 'alps' are flat, especially Mt Buffalo and Mt Bogong. Mt Feathertop is an exception as it has a sloping contour rising to a true peak and is readily recognised. As a family we never visited Mt Buffalo and its chalet. Perhaps my parents did and, if they did, they would have been impressed by the magnificent views of the Ovens Valley and of Mt Bogong in the distance.

The narrow Ovens Valley just south of Freeburgh in 1966
Mt Feathertop in the distance

I was also unaware that it was at Mt Buffalo where snow skiing was first popularised in Victoria. Skiing was taught by staff at the chalet from when it first opened and in 1931 the first mechanical tow rope was installed at Dingle Dell on Mt Buffalo. An artificial lake was created near the chalet and guests could go ice-skating in winter. I was not to encounter snow until the winter of 1950; by then we had moved higher into the Victorian alpine country.

2

A Gold Dredge in my Backyard

I lived at Freeburgh for the first nine years of my life. Our family home was the school teacher's residence situated alongside the small single room Freeburgh School. The residence was a simple three-bedroom weatherboard house with a corrugated iron roof. That roof brings back memories of heavy rain pounding on the roof at night while I lay secure in my bed. The school and house were fenced off but most of the surrounding land was either unfenced or was public property. Thus my siblings and I had one of the biggest 'backyards' one might imagine.

For all those nine years, we shared this 'backyard' with the Freeburgh gold dredge which slowly worked its way up and down the river flats of the Ovens Valley. The Ovens Valley here is narrow and at no point is more than a kilometre wide. The dredge was never more than a kilometre or so from our home and at times was very close. The dredge worked nonstop for six days per week and was closed down only on Sundays, when in those distant days Sunday was a day of compulsory rest.

Early in the last century, there were reported to be forty gold dredges in the Ovens Valley, spread out between Wangaratta and Harrietville but by the 1940s, there were only two, the one at Freeburgh and a larger one at Harrietville, the Tronoh dredge. It was claimed that the Tronoh dredge was the largest in the southern hemisphere. Both dredges were owned by companies listed on the stock exchange. As a child I was unaware of any of the business side of dredging but one can find that the financial pages of the newspapers in the 1940s regularly carried reports of how both dredges were faring. The Freeburgh dredge had commenced operation in 1940, although there had been another dredge at Freeburgh in the first decade of that century. Across the road from the Freeburgh school there was a deep pond that may have been left by that earlier dredge.

The gold dredge at Freeburgh circa 1948

Gold dredges were large noisy contraptions. They floated on pontoons built for the purpose. They were extremely damaging to the environment, primarily because they disfigured the landscape but also because they were usually steam-driven and thus required a steady supply of local timber to burn to generate steam. They also required a supply of water on which to be floated as well as needing a continuous flow of water for operating the sluices of the dredge. For the

Freeburgh dredge, the water came from the Ovens River via a culvert that had been constructed with its origin higher up the valley. The culvert ran immediately behind the school grounds. We called it our 'ditch'. The ditch provided us with some diverse activities. In addition, an unburied small bore metal pipe had been laid between the ditch and the school teacher's residence to supplement the only other water supply we had which came from our one large rain water tank.

That ditch was truly in our backyard as it formed the fourth border of the grounds on which stood the school and the teacher's residence. There was no fence on that fourth side. At that point the ditch ran along the beginnings of the foothills to the Victorian Alps and was approximately three to four metres above the level of the school playground. The elevation allowed water to be syphoned from the ditch via the pipe; I think that we used the water for baths, laundry and the large vegetable garden that my father created.

At one point, an area below the ditch was well-grassed with a moderately steep slope down into the school ground. We found that by using buckets of water, we could turn this grassy slope into a fast slippery slide. We had great fun. Prolonged use turned it into a mud slide; then our mother was not impressed.

As the Ovens River was well-stocked with rainbow trout, this fish readily found its way into our ditch (and our diet). We caught them by several means, including a line and hook, with earthworms for bait (at times the line was illegally left in overnight), tickling for them and, sadly, just picking them up from shallow puddles when the dredge owners temporarily closed off the ditch for some reason. As a boy I assumed that rainbow trout were native to Australia. It was many years before I learnt that they were an introduced species – coming from the west coast of the USA in 1894.

Gold dredging caused enormous physical damage to the local landscape. The buckets of the dredge dug deeply into the valley soil and when the dredged earth had been mechanically sluiced via a series of water-washed filters on the dredge, the soil, sand and stones were deposited behind the dredge to create what were called the tailings. The two most noticeable aspects of the tailings were first, that the top soil was now at the bottom and the visible surface was made of smooth river rocks and sand; and second, that the disturbance of the land resulted in tailings of the Freeburgh dredge that were a metre or more above the original ground level.

The Freeburgh dredge only dug down to around twenty feet (six metres) while the larger Tronoh dredge at Harrietville dug far deeper into the earth, to 130 feet (40 metres). As a result, the height of the Tronoh tailings was closer to three or four metres. I can recall seeing those tailings from a car window as a child of about six and was deeply impressed as to how much higher they were when compared to the tailings of 'our' dredge.

The Freeburgh dredge had a couple of long-lasting impacts on me. I often went to watch the dredge operating and was fascinated by how some loosened topsoil would crumble into the water as each dredge bucket moved on. This image then translated into a childhood nightmare where I would regularly dream that the earth on which my bed sat was crumbling into the water and that I and my bed were soon to follow.

I can now only recall that the men who worked the dredge were pleasant towards a young boy who took an interest in the dredge so I was surprised when later in life my younger sister told me the following story. She remembered a day when one of the workmen took me on to the dredge to show me how it all worked. She also recalled that he took me to a high part of the dredge and pretended that he was going to throw me overboard. She told me that she rushed home to alert our mother. I can vaguely recall being shown over the dredge, including being shown how the sluices functioned, but have no memory of being threatened in this way.

I did not know this then but the Tronoh dredge at Harrietville was also new. It was constructed over two to three years from 1940. There must have been some environmental consideration by the government of the day as the Tronoh dredge was obliged to first remove the top soil ahead of the dredging, such that in due course the top soil could be restored. In addition, the Tronoh dredge was powered by electricity provided courtesy of the State Electricity Commission. The dredging company must have had private power lines because neither the Freeburgh School nor the teacher's residence had electricity connected by the time we left the district at the end of 1949. I did not recall this but I have recently noted in newspaper records that in 1947 the Freeburgh dredge was converted to be powered by electricity.

To accommodate the path of the Freeburgh dredge, the Ovens Valley Highway was at times temporarily diverted. The highway in those days was unsealed so this was a simple task involving a bulldozer and a grader. The bulldozer was also used to level the tailings. I enjoyed watching the bulldozer at work. An outcome of my enjoyment was a gift of a toy metal bulldozer from Santa Claus one year.

To restore the environment, the Freeburgh dredging company planted pine trees over the tailings, thereby creating another industry for the Ovens Valley. Those pine plantations on the river flats are long gone but this secondary industry was such a success that the foothills to the mountains surrounding the nearby township of Bright are still the site of pine plantations. The restoration of the river flats is such that now the passerby could not imagine what the valley looked like in the 1940s. The only residual evidence of gold dredging is the occasional large 'waterhole', the final resting place of a decommissioned and disassembled dredge. One such water hole is a hazard on the golf course at Bright. Another is the large deep swimming hole at Harrietville, from where the Tronoh dredge was disassembled and relocated by the London-based company, Tronoh Mines Ltd, to mine for tin in Malaysia, it was reported.

While the Ovens Valley now appears restored to its original beauty, it may well be that any farmer who seeks to till the soil of the river flats near Freeburgh will encounter surface stones that before the gold dredges arrived would have been two to three metres or more below the top soil.

In my childhood I was unaware of any economic, environmental, political or other issues surrounding gold dredging. Neither can I recall if my politically aware father had any views on the pros and cons of gold dredging. Thus I have found it fascinating to trawl through the newspaper reports about gold dredging in the Ovens Valley in those years. In the 1930s there were unsuccessful protests from the residents of the region at the granting of mining leases for proposed dredging operations. The areas selected for dredging were the result of extensive drilling tests.

The war years were difficult for the dredges as in 1943 the Freeburgh dredge ceased operating for three years because of a shortage of labour and timber. My primary conclusion from these searches of the old newspapers is that investors' returns from the dredging operations (of both the Freeburgh and the Harrietville dredges) were never large and were variable as in some years losses were reported. By the mid-1950s, both dredges had closed down.

3

A Bush Education – The Beginning, at Freeburgh

Most of my primary school education took place in three different single-room bush schools and almost all of it was delivered by my father. There were no kindergartens in the bush so I began attending the Freeburgh School in 1944 at the age of three and a half. I doubt that this was a formal decision taken by my parents. It probably came about simply by my following my older siblings on the fifty yard (forty-five metre) walk from our home to the school. There is a photo that confirms my attendance. I am seated in the centre of two rows of pupils who numbered only eleven. Five of the group were girls from the same family. Their parents were migrants from Greece who ran an apple orchard and a small general farm on the eastern side of the Ovens River about a mile and a quarter from the school. The girls had a younger brother who was my age but because of the distance those girls had to walk to school each day, he did not start school until he was six. One of the girls was in Grade Seven or Eight.

At that time, bush school teachers were obliged to teach up to Grade Eight. Students could leave school after Grade Eight and, if they completed that grade satisfactorily, they were awarded the Merit Certificate. If their parents had so wished, those girls could have moved on to the school at Bright which was called 'a higher elementary school', but I don't think any of them did. On a single campus, the Bright School taught from Grade One through to Form Four (year 10 in modern terminology).

The total enrolment at Freeburgh in 1944

At Freeburgh every pupil sat in their allocated desk for each school day and the desks were arranged in rows such that the various 'classes' were separately identifiable. This was probably unimportant at Freeburgh when the enrolment was small but must have been helpful to my father at his next school where the enrolment was around thirty pupils. Each desk held two pupils. Made of timber, the desks were a universal design used in every school that I attended. The wooden bench seat and its wooden back rest were fixed to the desk. The desk had separate lidded compartments for each student, where one's books, pencils, pencil sharpener and twelve-inch ruler were stored. The lid was hinged at the front and sloped down towards one's midriff when seated. At the front edge of each desk was a flat area where pencils that were not in use could be placed and where there sat two small china inkwells.

To be promoted from the use of a black-lead pencil to using pen and ink (and blotting paper) was a big step. I don't recall achieving this at Freeburgh. For those allowed to use a pen, the teacher had to regularly refill each inkwell from a large bottle of dark blue ink. The pen used then had much more in common with the original bird's plume (the quill pen) than with modern fountain pens and ballpoint pens. The curved and hollowed open nib of the pen held little ink and the pen had to be dipped into the inkwell after every three or four words had been written. Accidents were frequent. Mothers may not have appreciated their child's promotion as ink had tendency to get on to school clothes and was difficult to wash out.

In front of the rows of desks sat a raised long platform and a desk and chair for the teacher. Behind the platform and the teacher's desk was a large blackboard which extended to almost the full length of that wall. The blackboard was in constant use and the teacher needed to have the skill and speed to write clearly in chalk. While white chalk was the most commonly used colour, many other colours were available. Older students were rostered to 'clean the blackboard' when needed. Sometimes the chalk made a very unpleasant squeaking sound when applied to the blackboard, a sound that I well recall and might best be described as 'sending shivers up your spine'.

The only light for the classroom at Freeburgh was natural, coming via an array of windows that made up most of the southern wall opposite the entrance hall. The timber structure of the school was stabilised by two strong metal rods that ran from the top of the front wall to the top of the back wall. Above our heads and above those rods was a cathedral roof.

When we first arrived at Freeburgh, the school had inadequate heating (a large fireplace) so in the cold winter months my father would have all the class do some indoor physical exercises for the first ten minutes each day to warm up both the pupils and the room. He managed to convince the Education Department to provide better heating and in 1946 a 'Warmray' brand slow combustion stove heater was installed in the front section of the class room. Its narrow flue ran up to the cathedral ceiling. The heater worked well but was yet another fire to be lit each day and for which wood had to be chopped.

Two remarkable events occurred at the Freeburgh School during the years that I attended. The first took place one morning when all the students had assembled in the school room waiting for the teacher to arrive. A few minutes before the official starting time of 9.00 am in came our teacher in his dressing gown, pyjamas and slippers! The children were astounded. What on earth was happening? Well, the answer lay with my father's brother, Uncle Vincent, who had travelled from Melbourne to stay with us for a short holiday. Vincent loved to play practical jokes. He was only a year younger than my father and was extraordinarily similar in appearance, so much so that most people assumed that they were identical twins. Aware of this similarity, Vincent had snuck out of our house in his nightwear and timed his appearance in the class room a few minutes before the real teacher arrived.

The other remarkable event related to our family's dog, Nip, a beautiful black part Kelpie with a gentle nature. Nip was safe with the school children and spent much of her day time in the school grounds. In those days, one of the banes of any teacher's working life was the unannounced arrival of the district school inspector. My father had little respect for inspectors generally and zero respect for the current local one, a Mr Jimmy Davidson. One day, Mr Davidson arrived unannounced at the school gate while the teacher and pupils were in class. Our lovely dog took one look at Mr Davidson and, deciding that he was unwelcome, grasped him by his ankle. The loud yells of fear soon brought help for Davidson. I suspect that any report that Davidson wrote from that visit would not have been favourable. The story was told and retold and Nip became famous in the Freeburgh district. The behaviour was out of character for Nip. She was an intelligent dog and I wonder now if she had sensed my father's deep antipathy to Davidson.

Much of our class time at Freeburgh was spent on reading, writing and arithmetic. We were expected to know our twelve times tables by heart from an early age. A copy of the tables was printed on the back cover of all the exercise books in which we wrote. The fact that twelve times twelve makes one hundred forty-four is deeply imprinted on my mind. Knowing one's twelve times tables was essential for daily living. Everything then was measured by the imperial system. There were twelve pennies to a shilling and twelve inches to a foot. Australia did not change to decimal currency and the metric system until 1966.

Each grade used a level-appropriate 'Reader' issued by the Education Department. Many of the short stories and poems in those readers remain in my memory. I could not tell you from which reader any story or poem came but Dorothea McKellar's 'My Country' which begins with the memorable words 'I love a sunburnt country' was one of the poems. Some of the stories were a little bloodthirsty as for example the story of the 'Hobyahs'. An amusing story, I think perhaps translated from the French, was entitled 'Blanchard's Trousers'. Blanchard as husband and father was a martinet who told his wife and daughters that if his new trousers, which were a little long for him, had not been taken up by next morning there would be trouble. During the night each family member quietly and separately came downstairs to take the trousers up. By next morning Blanchard found that his new trousers were now very short.

As radio reception in the Ovens Valley was virtually non-existent in the day time, the teacher had no access to the radio programs from which most other schools benefitted. The school did not have a record player or any musical instruments other than the simple tonette; this instrument is now probably better known as the recorder. Nevertheless, we pupils were taught to sing a few songs.

Primary school teachers were expected to teach about health matters. My father had some favourite health messages that we learned. Here are three that I recall:

> If you cough or if you sneeze,
> Always use a hanky please

> Wash your hands before a meal,
> No germs can come your health to steal

> Biscuits, lollies, cakes and such
> Never strengthen children much

This style of verse is called a distich. I have been unable to confirm that the ones above were created by my father, although I believe that they were. In relation to one's health, I also remember that he taught us to 'never put anything smaller than your elbow in your ear'.

My father did not believe in corporal punishment so the strap or the cane or even a ruler strike to the knuckles was never seen. The nearest he came to physical punishment was to push a pupil's head toward the desk top if their work was not satisfactory.

On the matter of health, because of the small size of our school and our remoteness from crowded streets, buildings, and public transport in Melbourne, I did not suffer any of the usual infections such as mumps, measles, German measles, chicken pox and infectious hepatitis during my childhood, with one exception. Neither was I at risk during the occasional outbreaks of poliomyelitis. This protective experience may have not been beneficial as I suffered chicken pox, German measles, infectious hepatitis and mumps (in that order) between the ages of sixteen and twenty-nine with unpleasant symptoms in each instance.

Another inventive approach that I recall my father using was in teaching us geography. He, perhaps helped by his older pupils, dug a map of Australia in the school grounds. This took the form of a relief in that the shape of Australian continent was left intact while the surrounding oceans were represented by excavation of the earth to around twenty-five centimetres. It was an effective way of showing that we were living on an island.

My father was keen to have his pupils read and was frustrated that the Freeburgh School had no form of library. He wrote to the Education Department every year requesting funds to establish a small library. Funding was made available in 1946 and with this he selected around 100 children's books, mostly written by Australian authors. The Education Department provided a tall timber book case to hold the collection. In March 1948, the school was closed as our enrolment had fallen below the critical number of seven. Nobody had left the district; the children had just become older. My two older siblings were now riding their bikes to school in Bright every day.

With the school closure my father was directed to teach at the nearby town of Ovens but our family was asked to continue to live in the teacher's residence; this situation applied until the end of 1949. After the closure of the school, my father wrote to the Education Department asking advice as to what he should do with his new library. The reply that came directed him to take care of the books until further notice. No such notice ever came – and my father did nothing to remind the Department. As a result, my younger sister (who became a librarian) still has some of those books. The tall book cabinet travelled with us over the next ten years. Then I stripped it of its shelves and turned it into a peculiar-looking wardrobe.

The Freeburgh school closure came when I was seven years old. The nearest school was at Bright but my parents decided that I was too young to be expected to ride six miles to school and six miles back – and besides I had not yet learned to ride a bike. Instead, I and my younger sister, Susan, were enrolled to be schooled by correspondence. Each week a large brown envelope containing new school work to be completed for that week would arrive in the mail. The envelope would also contain a previous week's work corrected and marked. The envelopes were stamped OHMS and the return envelope was addressed to the Correspondence School in Napier Street, Fitzroy. It was the first time I had heard of the inner Melbourne suburb of Fitzroy.

Our mother supervised our correspondence 'classes'. On most days we could complete the set work in an hour or so. On warm sunny days, our mother would place a folding card table out doors in the bright sunlight so these were indeed unusual school classes. With the school now closed, we had moved our cow in to feed on the long grass in the school grounds. I was not present on the day that our cow came to view my young sister's school work on the card table and knocked the table over, much to the fear and distress of my sister. My father was not there to assist us as he had been sent temporarily to teach at another school in the town of Ovens, a small town a few miles south of Myrtleford. This temporary appointment lasted until the end of 1949.

Lunch time at correspondence school

While our father came home every weekend, from Monday to Thursday he lodged in the hotel at Ovens. This arrangement required him to ride his bicycle to Bright early on Monday morning and catch the steam train that ran to Wangaratta. I think that the train must have stopped at Ovens as it would have taken a long time to walk to the Ovens school from the station at Myrtleford. On Fridays, he took the train back to Bright and then cycled home to Freeburgh.

I stayed for one night at the Ovens Hotel with my father. I think this came about because I needed to visit the dentist in Myrtleford. I have no memory of the dentist but I have a clear memory of eating dinner at a communal table at the Ovens Hotel. For the first course, everybody was served a plate of tomato soup. I had previously refused to eat tomato soup at home but, surrounded by strangers, I felt that I must eat it. I was surprised at how tasty it was!

My learning by correspondence was for less than a year. At the start of 1949 my parents now felt that at the age of eight, I was old enough to ride to Bright. I would be accompanied by my older siblings and there was almost no traffic on the Ovens Highway. But first I had to be taught how to ride a bike. The only bike we owned that allowed me to reach the pedals was one made for girls. I baulked at this at first and tried to show my parents that I might be able to ride a boy's bike by putting one leg under the cross bar. Of course, the physics involved made this impossible so my parents were very tolerant to even let me have a try. So a girl's bike it was.

That bike had some features that soon gave me trouble. It had been repaired and made into a 'fixed wheel' bike: this meant that it could not coast downhill without the pedals turning continuously. The bike had no brake (pedal or hand operated); instead, you stopped the bike by preventing the pedals from turning. In addition, I was still quite short so that when I sat on the seat of the bike, my feet did not maintain continuous contact with the pedals. This meant that when using the pedals to brake, I was standing upright on the moving pedals. The road to Bright was gravel at first and then sealed for the last two miles. It was flat and very gently downhill as the road closely followed the path of the Ovens River. The altered design of the bike was not likely to cause me difficulties on that road.

The girl's bike is on the right of this photo of Michael and me

Because I did not ride as quickly as my older brother and sister, I left well ahead of them to get to school on time. On my back was a small satchel which contained a simple sandwich for lunch; no student had a drink bottle; we drank tap water from the fountains at school. On Mondays, I also started out well ahead of my father who soon caught up with me. As he passed me, he would hand me a threepenny piece to spend in the Bright milk bar after school. I am proud that I never dropped the threepence. It was usually spent on a chocolate-flavoured milkshake.

In winter, the early morning cold made parts of my ride uncomfortable. The Ovens Valley is narrow with high surrounding hills and at least half of my morning ride saw no sunshine. I could always see the sunny spots ahead of me and the slight extra warmth when I rode into the sunshine was welcome.

I had only been at the Bright School for a few weeks when a new acquaintance who also rode part of the way home towards Freeburgh told me that he had found a shortcut from the school to the Freeburgh road. That sounded worth trying so I followed him one afternoon. The shortcut included a brief steep descent on a bumpy track, one that had been eroded by the rain. Half way down, disaster struck as my feet slipped off the pedals. Not only did I lose all braking capacity but I was now sitting on the continuously moving pedals as my bike completed the next twenty metres run down the descent. While I was very sore for a few days, I fortunately sustained no serious injury.

The ride home each afternoon was more difficult as now it was gently uphill all the way. At times a man with an empty tip truck would feel sorry for me. He would stop and lift my bike on to the back of the truck, then lift me into his high cabin and deliver me home. There were three tip trucks working this route, delivering sand to Bright and returning empty up the Ovens Valley for a new load. One kind driver always gave me a lift, a second did so occasionally, and the third never. When I heard a truck coming behind me, I was always keen to see which driver it was. I will never forget the kind driver's face nor his name. His name was Mr Les Moran.

The only danger on that road lay with the plovers during their long nesting season. Plovers mate for life and the male is highly protective and inclined to swoop on passing cyclists. I was never struck but I knew that I had to be on the lookout.

Closer to Bright there were several orchards whose boundaries were near to the road. There were so few children riding bikes on that road that the orchardists did not get upset if we stopped to take an apple or other item of fruit. One afternoon I stopped at an orchard to pick a ripe plum. They looked so appealing that I decided to pick a few more and take them home for my mother. I should have placed them in my school satchel that I carried on my back but instead I just quickly put them in the two pockets of my school shorts. It did not occur to me that this was unwise. When I arrived home, I rushed to tell my mother what I had for her. When I went to empty my pockets, I found that the ripe plums had turned to mush. I have never been able to face eating fresh plums since that day.

I did not enjoy the one year that I attended the Bright School. For me the school was too big and there were too many other pupils. Some of the games played at recess were violent with much older boys also being involved. One such game was called 'British Bulldog'. If you look it up in Wikipedia you will appreciate my concerns. I still have my school report from that year. It shows that I missed 18 days of schooling. Some of those days were when my mother kept me home because it was too wet to ride but I suspect that at times I must have also made other excuses not to go. I was happy with the news that my father had been posted to a new bush school, one that was small and where he would again be my teacher. I would be in fourth grade at this school.

4

A Bush Religious Education

My parents were both Catholic. They met via the tennis club at St Theresa's Parish in Essendon. My mother remained faithful to her religion all her life but my father gradually drifted away after an early phase of being a keen participant in the Melbourne-wide debating club of the Catholic Young Men's Society. Through my being born in the bush, my religious education was always going to be limited. Despite those limitations, I remained faithful until mid-life but then like my father I drifted away. I write now describing myself as a non-practising 'cultural' Catholic.

My baptism certificate shows that I was baptised at Bright in 1941 by Father Hussey and that my godparents were both women – two aunts who had travelled from Melbourne for the event. As we did not own a motor vehicle, we never attended Mass at the church in Bright. However, we were visited once a month by Father Hussey. He was based at Myrtleford and said Mass there and at Bright every Sunday. Once a month he also drove to Harrietville to say Mass. On his way back he called at our home in Freeburgh. It was my mother's task to set out our best crockery on our best tablecloth and provide Father Hussey with a cup of tea and a piece of cake. This was not a function at which children were welcome as I never participated and I have no memory of Father Hussey other than of his name. I do not know to where we were dispatched during each brief visit.

My next encounter with the religion in to which I was baptised was in the little town of Glen Valley to where we moved in 1950. In our first few months there we had no contact with the nearest priest who was based at Omeo, a town more than one hour's drive to the southeast on a narrow unsealed and dangerous mountain road. We still did not own a car so there was no question of the Breen family ever attending Mass at Omeo. Then a young married couple, Adrian and Patricia Black, came to live at Glen Valley with their one-year old baby, Tony. They too were Catholics and as there was another Catholic family nearby, now the priest at Omeo, Father O'Hay, accepted Patricia Black's invitation that he travel to say Mass at Glen Valley once a month. This he did and Mass was held in the lounge room of the small timber house in which the Black family lived on the other side of the narrow valley, opposite out home.

My parents soon became firm friends with Adrian and Pat Black. This was both inevitable and fortunate. Not only were they Catholic but their leftist political views aligned with those of my parents. Adrian was an accountant who had taken on the role of the manager of the local gold mine. He was a tall, handsome and well-educated man who enjoyed a beer. He became my father's drinking mate on Friday nights and Saturdays at the Glen Wills Hotel located two miles away. His wife, Pat, had only recently completed her training as a nurse at St Vincent's Hospital in Melbourne. (This was the first time that I had heard of St Vincent's Hospital). She was a very good looking brunette and as a nine-year old I was entranced by her. She and my mother became lifelong friends.

With my mother, dressed for Sunday Mass at Glen Valley

The first communicants at Glen Valley, 1950

As a result of Father O'Hay's attendance for Mass, my parents decided that it was time for I and my younger sister to make our First Holy Communion. For this event, a young person needed to be 'prepared'. Preparation involved instruction in the Catholic cate-chism which I seem to remember had as its first question 'Who made the world?' Pat Black gave this instruction to my younger sister and I together with three children of the other Catholic family in Glen Valley. We five thus made our First Holy Communion in the Black family home on a cold spring Sunday morning in 1950. The Mass was followed by a 'Communion breakfast' in their home.

While we did walk three miles to Mass occasionally from the next small town to which my father was transferred after the short time at Glen Valley, the instruction provided by Pat Black was to be my total exposure to a Catholic education until I was sent to a Catholic board-ing school in 1955. There in the first few weeks of Form 3 (year nine) I was given the cane for not knowing the catechism off by heart!

5

The Life of the Bush School Teacher

Teachers in Australian bush schools needed to be resourceful and resilient, as did their spouses*. In the case of my parents, their upbringings may have helped prepare them for the many demanding roles involved. All told, my father taught as the only teacher in eight single-room bush schools. These were, in order, at Arawata, Coromby, Lubeck, Ocean Grove, Freeburgh, Glen Valley, Yarrambat and Greenvale between 1929 and 1955. His longest stint was at Freeburgh. He married in 1934 while teaching at Coromby.

My father was raised on a wheat farm near St Arnaud. He was the fourth child of a family of twelve. He lived on the farm until he was twelve. He was used to physical work and handling horses. Surprisingly he never became a handyman around the house but was happy to do the physical work required to create and look after a large vegetable garden at most of the places where we lived. He was also willing to chop the firewood, a never-ending task.

My mother's upbringing was different. She was raised at North Essendon where the family home was truly on the outskirts of Melbourne. She and her siblings often played in empty paddocks where

---

* In that era, almost all teachers in government schools were men as women teachers were obliged to resign if they married. In Victoria, this applied until 1956.

the Essendon aerodrome now sits. Her resilience came from a different quarter. When she was ten, her mother died from tuberculosis. She was the oldest girl in a family of two boys and two girls so she was given responsibility from a young age. Those responsibilities increased when her carpenter father collapsed and died in the street when she was only twenty. Her sister was then fourteen and her younger brother was sixteen. So in their different ways my parents were well-prepared for many aspects of a challenging life in the bush.

There were many difficult and unpleasant tasks. At every school, the teacher was responsible for keeping the school and the school grounds tidy. He was also responsible for maintaining the girls' and boys' toilets. None of the toilets were connected to a sewer or even based on 'septic tanks'. Each had a toilet can that needed to be regularly emptied and buried as there were no 'night carts' in these remote rural areas. And my father had to do the same with the family's outdoor toilet at every school residence other than the last one at Greenvale. Here we had a septic tank and the novelty of an indoor toilet. For the first time we also had electricity! My father must have disliked the toilet task. He was capable of being angered by many things but I can't recall him ever complaining about this task or seeking to avoid it.

The work of the teacher in the class room was also demanding. It is difficult now to imagine how a sole teacher can set work for six and at times eight separate levels of pupils, keep each age group interested, and keep discipline. For a bright child, this may have been a good environment in which to learn as the child could not avoid being exposed to more advanced material. In most of these bush schools, the parents of many of the children were farmers or labourers who would themselves have had a limited education so that little help in education could be expected from the home.

In the bush schools with larger enrolments, the teacher was authorised to employ a part-time assistant who was given the title of 'sewing mistress' but who in reality was a teacher's aide. This role I am sure was created by the Education Department to provide paid work for the teacher's wife and thereby help to keep married teachers in the bush. My mother took on this role in at least three of the schools. This experience served her well as much later in life she was employed as a full-time teacher in a Catholic primary school in northern Melbourne (with a class of seventy pupils!) without ever attending a teachers' college.

The formal preparation of young teachers in Victoria when my father began his career was very different to that of today. In 1924, as a sixteen-year-old not long out of school, he was employed as trainee teacher at a primary school in Glenroy. After four years there he enrolled for formal training at Melbourne Teachers' College, situated on the campus of the University of Melbourne. This was a one-year course for both primary and secondary teachers. He graduated close to the top of his class. On graduation he was qualified to teach on his own. He opted for the bush because the pay was a little better. His first school was at Arawata in Gippsland.

Daily life for the teacher and his wife was not easy, particularly the lives that I observed at Freeburgh and Glen Valley. Neither house that we lived in had electricity so every night kerosene lamps had to be lit. We had no refrigeration. We had an ice chest but this was used as a small cupboard as there was no supply of ice. Limited cooling of foods in summer was possible through the use of an outdoor Coolgardie safe which worked by evaporative cooling. The safe was usually suspended from a nearby tree. At Freeburgh, the nearest shops were six miles away at Bright. We did not own a car so shopping was mostly done once a week on a Friday when a bus came from Harrietville in the morning and brought my mother home in the afternoon. Planning a weekly menu must have been tricky.

Cooking was done on top of, and in the oven of, a wood-fired stove which had to be lit every morning and kept going all day. A blackened kettle of hot water was kept on the side of the stove and could be moved to the centre when boiling water was needed for a cup of tea. We never drank coffee at home then. The weekly washing was done in a large copper which also had to be heated by wood fire. We had a bath every Sunday night and this too required wood to heat the bath water via a Malley chip heater. Kindling and fire wood supplies had to be maintained. Firewood could be purchased by the cord but still needed axe work to produce small logs for the stove. We all learnt to use an axe from a young age. My enthusiasm for wood chopping created a problem for me one day.

Water supplies had to be carefully watched as our single large rainwater tank could run low in summer. The tank stood on an elevated stand and a pipe provided gravity-fed cold tap water to the kitchen sink. The tank was an attractive place for mosquitoes to breed and many a time we found 'wrigglers' in our drinking water. Mosquito breeding could be discouraged by adding a fine layer of kerosene to the top of the water in the tank. We obtained some additional water via a pipe that ran from the culvert serving the local gold dredge. The culvert at that point was a few metres above the level of the school ground. This water supply was used for baths, washing clothes and watering our vegetable garden.

As was the case for all the residents of Freeburgh, we sought to be self-sufficient in terms of how we lived. We had a 'chook shed' at the back of the school yard. The hens were free to roam the entire school grounds. This created one of the two occasions when my father was very cross with me. One day, my younger sister and I were playing at 'cowboys and Indians' after school. As a 'cowboy' I had a desire to round up some cows; our hens seemed to fit the bill. Our father saw me chasing them and was very cross indeed, telling me that because of my actions, the hens were likely to not lay their eggs.

I was too young to know when we purchased our own cow to provide us with daily milk but we owned a cow for all the years that I remember at Freeburgh. Our cow was given the name of Judy. This name may have been connected with the birth in 1939 of my mother's first niece, Judith. Judy was a reliable source of unpasteurised milk. There were times when we had too much milk and then our hand-operated 'separator' came in to action to make butter. Without the modern machines, milking cows was a demanding physical task which had to be done twice a day. This task fell to my mother, every day of the week. At times, I sought to assist her but my technique was poor and my young hands were not strong enough.

In 1949, when we were getting ready to depart from Freeburgh, our cow Judy has left me with an inerasable memory. Judy was kept in an adjacent paddock separated from the school grounds by the culvert that took water to the gold dredge. My father had arranged to sell Judy and the buyer was soon to arrive to take her. She must have sensed that something was awry as she led my father a merry dance.

At one point in the chase, my father tripped on something, did a full somersault, and continued the chase. Luckily for my father he was running parallel to the culvert. That was the last time that we owned a cow, probably to the relief of my mother.

At Freeburgh my father established a large vegetable garden. There he grew potatoes, pumpkins, onions, cabbages, carrots, lettuces and tomatoes. This supply of food was supplemented in season by our foraging for items that included blackberries, mushrooms, chestnuts and walnuts. Early settlers had planted chestnut trees and walnut trees and many of these now stood on public land around the district. Roasting chestnuts on a large fork thrust into our open fire in our living room at Freeburgh remains a strong memory.

The author is on the fence. The Freeburgh vegetable garden is in the background

Blackberries were also introduced by early settlers and blackberry bushes were everywhere. A local woman supported herself in part by picking blackberries and sending them by road and rail to a jam manufacturer in Melbourne. She shipped the blackberries in kerosene tins; these were readily available as all the local households purchased kerosene in four-gallon tins for their lamps and sometimes for cooking on a Primus stove.

A regular source of meat for our evening meal was rabbit, roasted or in a casserole. My mother was an excellent cook and there was plenty of variety in our diet. We ate a lot of roast lamb and any leftover meat was ground for shepherd's pie. Another source of meat was tinned ham, a method of providing food first introduced by the military. The brand name that has stayed with me was 'Wham'. Fridays were difficult for Catholics in the bush for, without a refrigerator, storing fresh fish was not possible. We mostly ate salted preserved fish on Fridays. As mentioned, we had a hen house with as many hens as we needed. The hen house sat in the school ground and, as those grounds were fenced, the hens were let out in daytime to wander around the large school ground. We were never short of eggs.

Our hens met another need – what to have on the table for our Xmas meal. In the 1940s, if turkey was Xmas fare in Australia, this would have been restricted to the wealthy. We never ate chicken during the year but for Xmas one of our older hens was sacrificed. Using a sharp axe and a chopping block, my father would behead the old hen. That was the end of his duty as my mother, later aided by one or more or her four children, would immerse the dead hen in hot water for the painstaking task of plucking off all of its feathers. It was also my mother's task to gut the bird. Some readers may remember the term 'old boilers'. This was a reference to aged hens as the flesh was tough unless the hen was cooked for a long time.

My mother preserved fruit using the Fowlers Vaccola brand jars and seals and she made tomato sauce from the tomatoes that my father grew in his large vegetable garden. She also made delicious blackberry pie and apple pie as well as sponge cakes including lamingtons. For birthdays and Xmas she baked a fruit cake. Rarely, we ate ice cream brought home from Bright, insulated in a newspaper wrapping. The insulation effect was limited and the trip home by bicycle was slow so we usually ate a soft mush. In the depths of winter we sometimes made flavoured ice blocks. On a winter's evening my younger sister and I would add chocolate flavouring to milk and pour this into small metal cake pans. These were then left outdoors overnight and next morning we had our flavoured ice blocks.

For our two dogs, there was never any purchase of commercial dog food. They were fed with scraps including the bone of the leg of lamb. They both had shiny coats and were very healthy.

My mother was also very capable with her treadle-operated Singer sewing machine. I doubt that until I went to secondary school that I was ever dressed in clothes other than the ones she had made for us. She also enjoyed knitting and our pullovers were usually her work. I spent a lot of my time around my mother, watching her at her tasks and assisting when I could. I was fascinated by the skill of knitting and begged to learn how to do this.

When I turned nine, I was allowed to knit an item of my own choice. I chose to knit red and black long football socks. My mother ordered the wool, a pattern, and the right sized knitting needles from a shop in Wangaratta and off I went. I made good progress until I arrived at the tricky step of 'turning for the heel'. Here my mother assisted. The socks were a proud achievement for me. However, when I put them on, it immediately became clear that I was yet to master the skill of keeping the same tension on the wool throughout the knitting process. Through the wild variations in the tension applied, the socks bulged out in places where they should have bulged in. I think that my mother was happy that I claimed all the credit for the work. I never tried my hand at knitting again.

My mother had other skills. Until I was sent to boarding school at the age of thirteen, I had never had my hair cut by anyone other than my mother. There was a barber (cum-tobacconist) at Bright who probably cut my father's hair, but never mine or my brother's. My mother probably cut her own hair but of this I am uncertain.

My mother regularly attended meetings and events held by the Bright branch of the Country Women's Association and she had at least one very good female friend at Freeburgh who gave her help when needed. That friend came to care for me when my younger sister Susan was born, also at the Bright Bush Nursing Hospital, in 1944.

Our family visited Melbourne to see relatives in the summer holidays but this was not every summer. For one of those visits we exchanged houses with a school teacher in Brunswick. I have a memory of only one visit. By joining the Melbourne-bound train at Wangaratta, it could be difficult to find a seat. The train came from Albury and was bringing holiday visitors from Sydney. The entire journey from Wangaratta might be spent sitting on a suitcase in a corridor.

During the war, my father spent one summer holiday in Melbourne working in a foundry at Newport. We all remained at Freeburgh. I don't know whether he did this as part of the community 'war effort' or simply to supplement his income. The evidence of his participation, a sturdy pair of protective boots, sat at the bottom of his wardrobe for many years.

One Christmas holidays, my mother took me and my younger sister to Sydney by train to visit her sister and her sister's four daughters who lived at Sans Souci, a suburb on Botany Bay. I must have been seven years old. The trip began early in the morning on the bus that ran from Harrietville to Wangaratta. There we joined the Spirit of Progress steam train to take us to Albury. As this was still the era of the NSW and Victorian trains running on different gauge tracks, the train for Sydney was waiting for us on another platform. It departed Albury at 8.00 pm and was an all-night trip. We sat up all night. If there were sleeping carriages, we could not have afforded these. The stay with my Sydney cousins for two weeks was a remarkable new experience for a boy from the bush. It began badly as the family home was locked and the family was away in the Blue Mountains. There had clearly been a miscommunication. Luckily the next door neighbour believed my mother's story and helped us break into the house. My uncle, aunt and four cousins arrived back a couple of days later.

Turning to the professional aspects of the life of a bush teacher, I think that my father was an inventive teacher who found ways to draw his pupils into learning, using whatever material he had at hand. As mentioned earlier, from my first few years I could only recall minor elements of his approach to teaching but below I draw on an article written by my older sister that was published in the *Educational Supplement* of the *London Times* in 1969 to illustrate his approach. Her article was entitled 'Bush School'.

She was aged four when the family moved to Freeburgh so this was the only primary school that she attended and her father was her only primary school teacher. Here are selected aspects of what she wrote:

She introduced herself as follows:

'For many years I concealed the fact that I was first educated in a small "bush" school in a remote part of Victoria. I felt it an ignominious beginning and did not want to be known as "that girl from the bush".'

She went on to write:

'On Monday mornings we had the ceremony of raising the flag, when we all repeated in unison, "I promise to serve God, honour the King, and cheerfully obey my parents, teachers and the laws". We then sang "God Save the King", followed by "Advance Australia Fair". Such were the vestiges of the Empire.

Many lessons took place out of doors. We built feudal villages, made wigwams, igloos, gunyahs (for aborigines), boats and rafts. For nature study we strolled in the bushland looking at birds, butterflies, insects and plants, and then sketched them...

We did have some formal lessons such as spelling, arithmetic, and grammar, but I remember best our participation in creative activities. We always acted and recited at our end-of-year concert for the rest of the village, an audience of about thirty...

My father was very keen on athletics, especially when the combined schools' sports day was in the offing. The scoring was worked out on a percentage basis, so our small number of pupils was no handicap, especially as we all shone at sport. One year we came first. It may have been due to my father's training methods. He had us pole-vault-

ing, running, high-jumping, long jumping, relay running and playing team games long before the great day.

He even taught us the crouch start for sprinting, and we were the
only children who used it. When any of us won an individual cup
(which we did regularly each year) he was inordinately proud of this,
and talked about it for weeks afterwards.'

My sister's recollections are consistent with my later memories,
especially, as we will see, of the district school sports when we lived
at Glen Valley and of the activities my father encouraged his pupils to
engage in at my last bush primary school at Yarrambat.

Another responsibility that was usually allocated to the bush
teacher was to run the polling booth at the school on election-day
and to act as the returning officer for the Electoral Commission,
counting the votes after the poll had closed. At Freeburgh, the number of voters was small and it is likely that, as all the adults were well
known by my father, he could have guessed accurately for which party any vote was cast. My only memory of this work was that the votes
went into a well-worn locked wooden box which had been delivered
a few days earlier.

For most of the years that we lived at Freeburgh, my father had
written every year to the Education Department complaining about
the poor state of our small outdoor laundry building and requesting
that it be rebuilt. If approved, the request had to be passed on to the
Public Works Department which had its own schedule of works. The
end result was that a new laundry was built in 1949, well after the
school had been closed and not long before we departed. The builder
who had won the tender for the task was of course never going to

inform the Public Works Department of this changed situation. My father used this experience to increase his disdain for both the Education Department and the Public Works Department.

6

Possum Magic and Other Wild Life at Freeburgh

At Freeburgh, we encountered a range of wild life, including kangaroos, snakes, birds (magpies, kookaburras, rosellas and plovers), possums, echidnas and a plague of rabbits. I cannot recall sighting koalas or emus at Freeburgh. We sometimes saw wedge-tailed eagles soaring high in the blue sky. We had a 'pet' magpie for a few years. The magpie was partly tamed because we regularly fed him. We would find him every day perched on the paling fence that surrounded our house. He was given the name of 'Khaki', a somewhat surprising name as magpies are black and white. The name may have been a reflection of Australia's then involvement in World War 11.

That war was a long way away from Freeburgh. Its main effect on our lives was the rationing of basic foodstuffs that was introduced in 1942 and on the quality and range of gifts available at Christmas. As a school teacher, my father was not permitted to enlist. Several of his brothers served in the Army, a brother-in-law served in the Navy, another in the Army, and a childhood friend from St Arnaud drowned when the Japanese ship, the Montevideo Maru, carrying Australian prisoners of war, was sunk close to the Philippines by the US navy in 1942.

We had possums in the roof of our house and we heard them scurrying around almost every night. They did us no harm so we just accepted them. The house had been cheaply constructed. In our kitchen, the cupboard under the kitchen sink was open to the space that lay between the inside and outside components of the wall of that room. As a result, it was possible for our two resident possums to climb down from the roof via the hollow wall into that cupboard. Perhaps my mother left food for them. At the age of six I sought to tame these two possums. On a daily basis, I provided them with a saucer of milk and fragments of stale bread. They did not seem perturbed by my presence but I was never able to touch or handle them.

I decided that the pair needed to have names so I called them Peter and Paul. As a six-year old I was of course naïve. I think now that these names with their strong links to Christian history were prompted by the occasional attendance at our school of an Anglican minister who came to give us religious instruction. My choice of names needed adjustment when the proud parents brought their litter of baby possums to meet us at feeding time under the sink!

Snakes were a serious risk around the school and we were advised to always be on the lookout. If a snake was found within the school grounds, my father had no hesitation in killing it. Snakes are now a protected species in Australia. Perhaps they were in the 1940s but if so my father ignored the law. I recall that one summer he had a row of 12 or 13 dead snakes hanging on the strung wire fence at the front of the school. Should one wish to dispose of a dead snake, all you needed to do was to lay the carcass on top of an ant's nest. The carcass rapidly disappeared.

I had two close encounters with snakes at Freeburgh. In summer we often walked half a mile on a vaguely outlined track to a pleasant swimming hole in the Ovens River. Usually we went with my father to watch out for snakes. On this particular summer's day, my younger sister and I walked that track under the watchful eye of our older sister. When a large snake suddenly glided across the track in front of us, we all turned and hurried home, petrified. There was no swimming that day.

Very early in summer when snakes are emerging from hibernation they are sluggish in their movements. This probably accounts for my good fortune with my other experience. On the weekends and after school, we four children used the entire school grounds as our playground. The large area was well-grassed and never mowed so we mostly played in bare feet. One such day I was standing in bare feet near to the paling fence that surrounded our house watching my siblings at play. Suddenly my older sister called out to me 'Snake, Kerry, snake'. I looked down and saw at my feet a large snake. I rushed away to safety and can only explain my lucky escape on the effects of hibernation.

Our father told us an amusing story about kangaroos at Freeburgh. He recounted that he was riding his bicycle home from Bright at dusk. He perceived what he thought were two local residents chatting on the side of the road near to the home of a local family. As he neared them he said 'Good evening' only to be surprised to observe two large kangaroos hop away in different directions.

Rabbits were a big part of our lives. We hunted them, we ate them, and some locals made a living from them. The plague of rabbits in Australia may well have been at its apogee in the late 1940s. Most readers will be familiar with the best known account of when and why rabbits were brought to Australia from England. In 1858, a Mr Thomas Austin imported 24 rabbits from England with the intention of breeding them to have game to hunt on his large estate near Winchelsea in Victoria. They bred too successfully. The story is more complex than that but here is not the place to tell it.

While rabbits were a disaster for local farmers in the Ovens Valley and elsewhere, rabbits created business opportunities for others and were an important food source at times, especially during the Great Depression. There were few families in the Ovens Valley who did not regularly eat roast rabbit or rabbit stew. Catching rabbits was a favourite leisure activity of my brother who was six years older than I. Rabbits could be captured or killed by a number of means including shooting, trapping, ferreting and poisoning. My brother only employed ferreting and shooting. A woman neighbour made part of her living by trapping rabbits. A farmer neighbour laid poison bait for rabbits and my father blamed him when our second dog, a mongrel named Pincher, died apparently of poisoning.

I was allowed to participate in some of the ferreting excursions. These were whole day affairs. My brother owned three ferrets which had to be carried to the chosen venue in small homemade wooden boxes strung on his shoulders and on a shoulder of his best mate, Ian, who lived nearby. We also took with us a large supply of nets and pegs, a mattock, a box of matches, a sandwich lunch and our dog Nip. We never had more than a couple of miles walk to locate a suitably large rabbit warren.

The first task involved pegging netting over all the burrowed entrances to the warren. Once that was achieved, the ferrets were released into the burrows. Very soon the ferrets had the rabbits scampering from their warren into our nets. Occasionally we would find that we had failed to put a net over an exit but this was where Nip excelled. She would crouch at the highest point of the warren with an ear to the ground and thus was able to tell the direction that an escaping rabbit had taken. Should that rabbit appear at an un-netted exit, Nip was there to collect him.

I recall one very successful day where we came home with around forty dead rabbits. To be able to bring them home, my brother and Ian had to cut down two narrow saplings to create two poles to which the rabbits were tied by their feet. The poles were then mounted on the boys' shoulders with my brother leading the long walk home. Their work was not finished as now the rabbits had to be skinned and gutted and the skins mounted on wire frames for drying. They made pocket money from the skins.

Not every ferreting excursion was straightforward. A common problem was that one of the ferrets would trap a rabbit in the warren and eat it for 'lunch', followed by a post-prandial sleep. When this happened, our first step at retrieval involved trying to smoke the ferret out. The nets were replaced by bunches of eucalypt branches placed on all the exits to keep any smoke in the warren and a fire would be lit at one of the entrances to create smoke. When this failed, we had to resort to using the mattock to dig the ferret out.

At times we captured baby rabbits. We were not inclined to kill these small animals and instead would carry them home with the plan to feed them and keep them as pets. On arriving home, a rabbit hutch was then hastily put together with wire netting and timber. On not one occasion were there rabbits to be found in the hutch the next morning!

My brother was allowed to have a 22-gauge rifle at the age of 12 or 13 and he was sometimes successful at shooting a rabbit. An uncle in Melbourne sent him a much more powerful rifle as a gift. It was a US army automatic rifle with a magazine for 15 bullets and the bullets were close in size to those for a .303 rifle. It had a very good gun sight and was accurate over 300 yards. However, it was so powerful that if a rabbit was shot, the animal was barely recognisable. Only a limited supply of bullets came with the gift and more bullets were not able to be purchased. I don't recall what happened to that rifle.

Trapping of rabbits was banned in Australia in the 1980s because of the cruelty it involved but in the 1940s it was widely used. Sometimes the traps caught other animals including small pets. The neighbour who made part of her living through trapping rabbits and selling the skins to a Melbourne hat maker once took me with her while she checked and reset her traps. It was a memorable event as it took place well after dusk with only a little moonlight to guide us. The traps that she set were not visible as they were covered by a light layer of sand or loose soil. That layer needed to be placed in a gentle manner so as to not activate the metal jaws of the trap. What amazed me was that in the dark she unerringly recalled the exact places where she had set each trap on the previous night.

We sometimes also tried to trap native birds in the school playground with the idea that we could keep them as pets. Our method involved propping a wooden box up with a forked stick to which a long length of string was attached. Some grains of wheat were spread on the ground under the box and then we retired at a distance, concealed behind the trunk of a large oak tree, ready to tug on the string should a parrot or some other bird be tempted by the wheat. Luckily for the birds, they were always quicker than were we.

7

How we Entertained Ourselves

During my childhood, there was no television and, until I was six or seven, not even a radio in our home. Day time entertainment had to be self-improvised while evenings primarily were spent reading books or playing games of dice or cards.

A favourite outdoor game was a form of hide and seek called 'Kick the tin'. One child was chosen to be 'It' (the seeker) for the first round. He or she would be instructed to close their eyes and count out aloud to twenty before they opened their eyes again. The game began with one of the other players kicking an empty jam tin as far away as they could. That was the signal for every other player to run away to a hiding place in the school yard. 'It' had to replace the tin at the starting point before he or she went seeking the other players

'It' needed to find and tag each participant before they ran back to kick the tin. The further the seeker moved away from the tin to find and tag any player, the greater the risk that other well-concealed players would race to the tin before the seeker could tag them. We young children did not know it at the time but variants of this game have been played by children all around the world. You will find the details in Wikipedia if you search for 'Kick the can'.

Another game that we played in the school yard at two of the bush schools that I attended was called 'up and de over'. I think that this may have been invented by the children at the Glen Valley School as I have not been able to find evidence of it being played widely. It was very simple game that required just a free-standing large building (e.g. a small bush school), a tennis ball and as many children as could be found. Two teams were selected and moved to stand on opposite sides of the school. The game began when one member of one team threw the tennis ball over the school roof, calling out loudly 'up and de over' as the ball was thrown. For the throw to be in play, the tennis ball had to bounce at least once on the opposite side of the roof.

For the receiving team, it was vital that the ball was caught on the full. If it was not caught, then the team had to forfeit one member to the other side. The team would of course forfeit the child who was deemed to be their least reliable catcher. If the ball was caught, this was loudly announced and a chase around the school began. If the catcher of the ball could tag one or more of the opposition before they had completed a full circuit, then those tagged players had to join the other team. Tagging could be achieved by touching an opponent with the ball or throwing the ball accurately to hit the opponent.

The game continued with each team in turn throwing the ball over the roof to the opposition. It ended when one side had lost all its players or when the school bell rang. It was a fun game which could involve all ages, provided great exercise, and improved our skill at catching.

Other games that waxed and waned in popularity included marbles, skipping and hopscotch. Most children were too poor to own their own skipping rope but, at school, group skipping with a large rope turned by a child at each end was especially popular. It took skill and timing to enter the game once the rope was being turned.

At Freeburgh my older brother and sister and three or four other children around their age often played the game of 'paper chase'. This was played at the weekends as it took place over a wide stretch of the Ovens Valley and surrounding hills and not just in the school yard. Old newspapers were torn into small pieces and then stuffed in a large hessian bag. The hessian bags were readily to hand as these had originally held the feed that we purchased for our cow.

One of the group nominated as the 'hare' set off carrying the bag to lay the paper trail through the river flats and into the timbered foothills. The rest of the group followed the trail an agreed number of minutes afterwards as the 'hounds'. The aim of the game was first to not lose the trail and second to try to catch the 'hare' before he or she got back to the starting point.

I was never permitted to take part in a paper chase. This was a wise decision on the part of my parents as there were old open mine shafts in the nearby foothills and some of the foothills were so densely timbered that I may have become lost.

At each school that I attended, the school participated in the district sports held each year. Most of the events were for individuals (sprints, high jump and long jump) but there were also team events for which the teacher had us practise. One was the game of 'tunnel ball' played with a very heavy ball that was strangely called a 'medicine ball'. Another involved rapid passing of a netball between team mates lined up diagonally opposite to each other while the first member of the team dashed to the other end in time to receive the ball back and so on until every team member had been used.

Another opportunity to compete in athletic events came from the community picnics held in local towns. At one such picnic held at Harrietville when I was five, I became a 'professional' athlete. My parents entered me in an under six years 100 yard race which I won. The prize for winning was five shillings (worth 20 dollars now). While I have little memory of the race, I vividly recall that for some time my family teased me because I had won money I was now a 'professional' and was thus excluded from any future amateur event. Later in life I became aware that my mother had been a keen athlete who had competed for the Essendon Harriers amateur athletics club as a young woman. She might have been pleased with my win.

Night time or indoor games include ludo, snakes and ladders, and draughts (but not chess) as well as the card games of euchre and cribbage. In 1950 we were introduced for the first time to the new dice game of Monopoly. Euchre was a popular card game then for adults as well and my parents shared the hosting of euchre parties with neighbours in Freeburgh. Given the small population of Freeburgh, there were usually only two tables with four adults playing at each table.

Our favourite night time activity was reading. In winter this was with all the family sitting around the large fireplace in our living room. There we read by the weak light of a kerosene wick lamp while if we read in bed this was by candle light. Most of the books that we read were borrowed from the public library in Bright. We did hold a subscription to a weekly children's magazine, *The Champion*, which was published in London. It mostly contained short stories and serial stories with minimal comic strips and was keenly awaited. Our mail was delivered by the 'mail van' which took the mail to all the homes between Bright and Harrietville.

The Bright Library held few children's books so our parents would carefully choose adult books that we might enjoy. In my last year at Freeburgh, I recall reading Compton McKenzie's amusing tale, '*Whisky Galore*', a J B Priestley story of a travelling theatre company, '*Good Companions*', and an American western, '*The Virginian*', by Owen Wister. I have recently re-read them all and they remain excellent novels.

Our night time habits were altered in around 1946 when my parents purchased our first radio. It sat on a large sideboard in the living room. It was powered by a 12-volt car battery that sat alongside it. The battery was taken into Bright from time to time to be recharged. Radio reception in the Ovens Valley was poor and but was stronger at night. To improve reception, my father ran an aerial into one of the two large oak trees in the school yard. Even then, the only station that we could reliably receive was the ABC station 2CO which was based at Corowa in southern NSW. The Ovens Valley ran in that general direction so there were no mountains between Corowa and Freeburgh.

Station 2CO ran a children's half hour every afternoon at 5 or 5.30 pm. For the show, parents could write in to have their child's birthday announced on the radio. As part of the announcement, the birthday child would be told to 'follow the string'. A length of string had been laid earlier by the parents in and out of a couple of rooms until at the end of the string a birthday gift was to be found. For young children, having one's name announced on the radio was exciting.

Another well attended social activity were the regular dances held in the Freeburgh Hall. The Hall sat diagonally opposite the school on the eastern side of the Ovens Valley Highway. It was simple timber structure of one large room with an elevated stage at one end. Behind the stage was a small kitchen for preparing supper.

The Freeburgh Hall in 1966, since demolished

I do not know how frequently these dances were held or who organised them but it was my father's task to polish the dance floor a day so before any dance. He achieved this by first spreading candle wax shavings in every direction. Then the floor was polished with a hessian bag. To create some weight on the bag, either I or my younger sister were sat in a large wooden box positioned on top of the hessian bag. A rope was attached to the box and we towed each other up and down the hall until the floor shone. At times we were both in the box while our father did the towing.

The dance was always on a Saturday night and children were welcome to attend and to participate in the dancing, including the 'progressive barn dance'. This was a great opportunity for young children to observe how adults conducted themselves. An entrance fee was charged, presumably to pay the small band who provided the music and perhaps to raise money for some other cause. There was a break for supper and for the musicians to rest. In the kitchen behind the stage a four gallon 'kero tin' filled with water had been heating up over an open fire place so that tea and coffee could be offered. The coffee then came as a liquid mixture in a small brown bottle to which chicory essence had been added during manufacture. In addition, volunteers had made sandwiches for the supper.

During the evening tickets were sold for a raffle. At one of the dances, I held the winning raffle ticket (paid for by my parents). The prize was a colourful handmade cushion or pillow covered in silk. This dance must have taken place in late August as it was just before my mother's birthday on September 3. I gave my raffle prize to my mother as a birthday gift.

My assumption now is that there would have been an informal roster of dance nights among all the towns in the Ovens Valley that possessed a dance hall. These other towns would have included Harrietville, Bright and Myrtleford and possibly Wandiligong in a nearby valley. Such an arrangement would have provided regular work for the band members and explained why the Freeburgh dance was so well attended.

8

Activities with my Older Brother

My older brother Michael generally treated me kindly and allowed me to 'hang around' when he was engaged in a variety of activities with a local boy named Ian. Ian was the same age as Michael and they were close friends. When old enough, they rode together each day to the Bright School to attend the secondary classes. They remained in contact for the rest of their lives. As mentioned earlier, I was invited on some of their ferreting excursions.

Close by on the other side of the Ovens Valley Highway, directly opposite our house, was a deep pond. I am sure that it had once held a gold dredge. It was sometimes a place where my brother and Ian swam or paddled around on large flat logs that floated well. One day they decided that they would build their own 'canoe' for use in the pond.

They chose the building materials: a sheet of used corrugated roofing iron and some timber from the wooden packing cases that the local orchardist used. There were many obstacles in their path. The roofing iron, having been used, had many nail holes in it so first these had to be soldered over. The iron sheet was then folded length-wise to make the base and sides the canoe. Now each end of this structure needed to be made water-tight.

A log raft on the pond of an earlier gold dredge: my older brother aboard

They planned to seal the ends with the timber walls of the packing cases. The idea was feasible as there were no gaps in the packing case walls. However, because the roofing iron was corrugated, they struggled to make their craft watertight. There was an additional problem that defeated them as the exposed edges of the roofing iron were sharp, making getting in and out of the canoe hazardous. Nevertheless, they launched their 'canoe' a couple of times and sat in it trying to paddle away while the craft quickly filled with water. At that point, they lost interest and abandoned the task.

The vegetation around that pond created a minor problem for me. I must have been allergic to one of the plants around the pond as after spending time at the pond, the next day I would be troubled by itchy and sticky eyelids. This has never recurred and thus I do not know what triggered the reaction.

Thinking about that pond reminds me of a visit we had one Xmas holidays from some unruly second cousins. They came to stay for a week or so, brought from the Melbourne suburb of Essendon by their widowed mother (a first cousin to my mother). For my brother and I this became a very unhappy Xmas. My brother had been given a beautiful fishing rod for Xmas. One cousin, a year older than my brother, took it out to the pond and damaged it beyond repair. I had been given a long-pined for Hornby wind-up train set. Without my knowledge, another one of the cousins took my train set to the school sandpit and thereby destroyed the wind-up mechanism beyond repair. He was three or four years older than I. He grew up to be an amiable adult but I never forgave him for what he did to my train engine.

At the age of ten or eleven, Michael was given an air rifle. He used it a lot, practising his aim with empty jam tins set some distance away. He also aimed at the numerous birds in the trees of the school grounds, rosellas most commonly. I can't recall that he ever hit one which is fortunate. I begged and begged to be allowed to fire his air rifle and one day he said yes. To load up an air rifle with compressed air, one hand has to be held tightly over the tip of the barrel of the gun. While he was preparing the rifle in this manner, in my youthful enthusiasm I already had my hand on the trigger. Then I accidentally pulled the trigger and the small metal pellet that the rifle fired went directly into the palm of Michael's hand. Luckily for me it did not penetrate the skin but it must have hurt a lot as I learnt some new swear words.

My brother was happy to teach me how to bat at cricket, to kick a football, and to use a tennis racquet. Early in my batting lessons with Michael and Ian bowling to me, they both suddenly exclaimed 'hat trick!' To my great annoyance, they refused to explain to me what a hat trick in cricket was.

A small area of the school yard had a gravel surface which sat between two large oak trees. By tying a piece of string between the trees as a crude tennis net, my older brother and sister were able to play some tennis. Again, I was allowed to participate. I can't recall if either of my parents played tennis while we lived at Freeburgh. When we moved to our next bush school in 1950, there was an asphalt tennis court and my father organised a tennis tournament. Adults and children competed together. To enable some sought of parity, my father allocated handicaps to everyone. My handicap was 'love forty' which meant that I only had to win one point against an opponent on a scratch handicap and I had won a game. By now I was nine years old and I could get the ball back over the net so I must have won a few games. We played doubles tennis as well. I can't recall how the handicaps were adjusted for the doubles matches.

The tennis racquets we owned were made of wood and were strung with catgut. Metal frames and much larger racquet heads were decades away. We were taught to take great care to never leave a racquet outdoors in the weather as it was likely that the racquet head would warp and become useless. Even when kept indoors, racquet heads were stored in their own small wooden press to help prevent warping.

I was keen to practise my tennis skills but the only wall that I could use for this was the weatherboard wall of the school. The wall was constructed with the overlapping timber such that the rebound of the tennis ball was unpredictable. This may help to explain why later in life one of the strengths of my tennis was volleying at the net. Another mode of practice involved the purchase of a tennis ball with a length of strong elastic attached to it. The other end of the elastic was then tied to a house brick. You then hit the ball as hard as you could and ideally it would always rebound to be hit again. Unfortunately, at times the elastic would break and the tennis ball would fly off into the distance.

At Freeburgh in the summer months we were taken to the Ovens River to swim. This was usually after school so we went with my father who kept watch for snakes while my mother stayed home to prepare the dinner. It was a mile or so to walk to the chosen swimming spot. Here some large rocks slowed the river down a little, creating a pool. On our side of the river was a large flat area covered in smooth stones of varying sizes while on the opposite side, the river had carved its way into a steep hillside. I only learned to dog paddle there and never became a strong swimmer. When bored with swimming, we would compete to see who could skim the water with the smooth stones and count how many times the stone would bounce off the water.

My strongest memory of those summer walks to the river to swim is neither the walk nor the swimming but is the great appetite that I developed for my dinner after the exercise. My favourite meal then was shepherd's pie followed by blackberry pie. Closely linked to that memory of the walk for a swim is the scent of the Australian tea tree that lined the banks of the river. Whenever I smell tea tree now, it takes me back to Freeburgh.

In the one year that I attended the school in Bright with my older brother, he placed great trust in me. One lunch time he was drawn into a fist fight with a red-headed 'sworn enemy'. The fight seemed to go on for ages as no teacher appeared. My brother was acclaimed the winner by the watching fellow students but in the process he received a bloodied and broken nose. On the way home, he told me that he would give the following explanation for his injury to our parents. His story sounded believable as it entailed two cricket balls hit into the air at the same time. He planned to say that he caught one but, unaware that the other one was coming his way, he was struck on the nose. I do not know if our parents believed his yarn but I can report that his trust in me was justified as throughout my life I never told my parents about that fight.

The two large oak trees in the school grounds at Freeburgh were the basis of at least three other enjoyable activities. When they shed their leaves each year, it was our job to rake the leaves into a large pile ready for burning. Before they were set alight, we had the joy of running and jumping into the pile: the landing was very soft. In addition, the acorns from the oak trees provided ideal ammunition for our home-made sling shots. The sling shots were constructed from the forked branch of a eucalypt sapling and the rubber of the inner tube of a car tyre.

Burning those oak tree leaves brings to mind the celebratory bonfires that were held throughout Australia in that era. These were arranged for the evening of Empire Day in May and Guy Fawkes Night on November 5. On both occasions, as well has holding a bonfire, we enjoyed the fun of firecrackers. As a child I had little knowledge of the origins of Empire Day but now know that it was originated in 1903 as a celebration of the birthday of Queen Victoria who died in 1901. Empire Day was replaced in 1958 by Commonwealth Day, a day that Australia has chosen not to celebrate. Guy Fawkes Night had a much longer history but since the 1980s has been abandoned in Australia because of the frequency of serious injuries from fireworks. Fireworks are now banned throughout Australia other than in Tasmania and the Northern Territory. November 5 became known as 'cracker night', being an abbreviation of 'firecracker'. I enjoyed the pleasure of firecrackers not only as a child but even as a young adult and I regret the fact that irresponsible behaviour of a few people necessitated their banning.

The bonfires were also eagerly awaited. These were always community affairs and often held in the school grounds. For weeks dried timber and other materials that would burn well, including old car tyres, were collected and added to the pyre. For the Guy Fawkes Night bonfire, a stick figure in old clothes was mounted on top of the pyre to represent Guy Fawkes. Everyone in the district was informed of the starting time which was always after dusk. The bonfire was lit to loud acclaim and this was also the time to light the firecrackers.

In addition to the two old oak trees in the school grounds there were many deciduous imported trees planted in the Ovens Valley. When their leaves turned red or golden in autumn, the valley was additionally beautiful. From time to time, we would see an artist on the side of the highway with their oil paints, easel and a stool, working away at capturing this beauty. Around Bright in particular the autumn leaves still attract tourists.

9

Wood-choppers, Circuses and Other Diversions

During our time of living at Freeburgh, we regularly attended the agricultural show that was held each year at Bright. Our family usually attended for at least one day of the event. My clearest memory of these days was watching the wood-choppers in action. These men were competing for prize money. There was an informal circuit that competitive wood-choppers around Australia followed. The best-known name on the circuit then was Jack O'Toole*.

These men were muscular and proud of their physique. In competition they usually wore a tight white singlet, dark trousers and sturdy boots. The axemen competed in two different events. The timber that they had to chop through was newly collected eucalypt so it was relatively soft. In one event, a short log of about 45 centimetres in diameter was mounted firmly on the ground for each competitor and all that was required was for the log to be chopped right through as quickly as possible. They were so quick at this task that each heat only lasted a few seconds.

The second event (tree-felling) required more skill as now competitors faced eucalypt logs of around three metres in length which

---

* https://adb.anu.edu.au/biography/otoole-john-jack-15437

were mounted upright. The axeman had to make his way to the top of the log and then cut through its width entirely so that the top of the log fell to the ground. To make his way to the top, each man was given two solid planks. The axeman cut a notch in the log a metre or so off the ground, with the notch shaped to hold the first plank. Standing on this plank, he then cut another notch a metre higher to take the second plank. In this way, he worked his way up to a position where he could securely take on the task of lopping off the top of the log. This was exciting to watch.

As I had already learned how to swing an axe, I hastened home and sought to emulate these men. Around the school ground at Freeburgh, or more accurately just beyond the school ground fence, a large number of eucalypt saplings were growing. My father gave me permission to practice my wood-chopping skills on these young trees. I soon tired of this challenge; the timber was soft and the task too easy. So I looked around for a hardwood log to cut down and I found one standing upright in the school ground.

I had slowly chopped my way about half way through the log when my father saw what I was chopping down. It was one of the two posts that held up the netball rings for the school's netball court! He was very angry and, for the only time in my life, I was taken indoors and given a belting on my backside. My father was deeply opposed to corporal punishment so he must indeed have been cross. This was the end of my aims for a career in wood-chopping although I continued to contribute to chopping wood for our kitchen stove and our open fire place.

I also learnt how to replace an axe handle. Handles were inclined to break with repeated use. It was at times difficult to remove the old shaft from the metal axe head as it had been fitted so tightly. In this instance one had to burn the shaft out by placing the axe head in a fire. I was also taught how to sharpen an axe blade.

In Bright, and later when we lived at Yarrambat, we were taken to see travelling circuses. The feats of the trapeze artists and the tight-rope walkers fascinated me. I was not able to rig up a trapeze at home but I did find a low fence that seemed suitable for learning how to tightrope walk. The fence was approximately a metre high and had been built to protect a garden in the school ground. The top of the fence was made of 'four by four' timber mounted in such a way that one corner of the timber was uppermost. Thus the edge of the timber created a solid straight fine line, equivalent (in my young mind) to a tight wire.

I set out to practise walking on the fine line and thought that I was making some progress when suddenly I fell to the ground. Unfortu-nately, my left knee struck a sharp rock and I scampered home with the knee bleeding and me crying. My fall had created a nasty lacera-tion, one that today would have led to a trip to the doctor for sutur-ing but the nearest doctor was a long way away. My mother bathed the wound in a dilute solution of Dettol (the favourite antiseptic in that era) and bandaged it firmly. The wound became infected and it took weeks to heal. The only lasting benefit was that I now had a scar to record whenever I was asked to fill in a form about scars or other identifying features.

Other diversions at Freeburgh included rare trips to Bright to the movie theatre. If my memory is reliable, I was only taken once or twice. One film was entitled 'The Greatest Show on Earth' and was based on the US travelling circus of the Barnum and Bailey. The male lead was a young Burt Lancaster who played the part of a trapeze artist. In those days, the program would usually include a less well-publicised film screened ahead of the 'main attraction'. The only other film that I recall was entitled 'It Grows on Trees' and was a comedy based around the notion of a magical tree on which dollar notes grew. It may have preceded the circus movie. The movie theatre in Bright was only open at night and it may well be that it was on the trip home from that movie in a neighbour's car that we saw the flames of a bushfire burning on the peaks of the hills on the western side of the Oven Valley.

Although the distances were considerable, every year a combined schools' athletics carnival was held for the schools of the district. The schools involved not only included those in the Ovens Valley (Harrietville, Freeburgh, Bright, Ovens and Myrtleford) but also schools as far away as Beechworth. I cannot recall participating in a carnival while at Freeburgh; perhaps I was too young to go. However, I have clear memories of these events from our time at Glen Valley and at Yarrambat. At the latter two schools, the children were transported in open trucks and not in buses so I presume that this was also the case in the Ovens Valley.

Through dint of living in under-populated areas, I was denied the opportunity of participating in regular team sports or receiving early coaching in any sport. This situation changed a little when our family moved to Yarrambat in 1951. Here my older brother and sister played competitive tennis with the Plenty Tennis Club and my brother (who was talented at sport) played as the high-marking full-forward for the Diamond Creek football team in the Diamond Valley League.

My first opportunity for team sport was at Eltham High School. This experience led me to join the Under 15 Diamond Creek cricket team at the start of summer in 1954. Our practice sessions in the 'nets' were stressful as at the age of just thirteen, I had to pad up to the adult bowlers. I only recall one game with the Under 15's. It was a morning game in Eltham. I rode my bicycle to the Diamond Creek railway station and took a train to Eltham. My memory (which may be false) is that in batting I made a few runs. I was looking forward to a full season of cricket but this was not to be. Just before Christmas of 1954, my father was re-located to a school at Greenvale.

10
Medical Care in the Bush

This is a brief chapter as medical care in the Victorian bush was limited in the 1940s. In Bright there was a one-man medical practice and a small hospital called the Bright Bush Nursing Hospital. I was born in that hospital but in the next nine years I did not need to visit either the doctor or the hospital. I do recall that one day the doctor came from Bright to vaccinate all the children at the Freeburgh School. I think that the doctor's name was Dr Simpson. He arrived in a handsome large modern black car with a single fine red line drawn along the middle of the bodywork on both sides of the car. I also recall the shape of the tiny glass ampoules from which he drew up the vaccine. This must have taken place in 1946 or 1947 and I wonder now with what we were vaccinated. My best guess is that it was 'tetanus toxoid' used to prevent tetanus as most of the other vaccines that are now used to prevent the common viral illnesses had not been developed by 1946. Tetanus vaccine was introduced in 1924 but only became widely used during and after World War II.

In such a remote region of Victoria as Freeburgh, there was little exposure to the everyday viral infections that spread readily in cities. This probably explains why I did not contract chicken pox until I was sixteen, infectious hepatitis until I was twenty-five, and mumps until I was twenty-nine. The remoteness also protected us from the terrible epidemics of polio in Melbourne, the fear of which only faded with the introduction of the Salk vaccine in 1953. However, I did not avoid the measles as a child but that is a story for the next chapter.

I cannot recall any episodes of ill-health in our family in our nine years at Freeburgh. I do recall an unfortunate accident that befell a man who came to the school grounds at my father's request to deal with some tree branches that may have posed a risk to the students. I think that I witnessed the accident as I was intrigued by his work. He was high in an old tree situated near the student's toilets and was using a saw to lop off a branch. He had no safety equipment. Suddenly he lost his grip and had a nasty fall to the ground. I don't know if he was taken to the doctor in Bright but I was later told that he had suffered several broken ribs. He made a full recovery.

When we moved to Glen Valley in 1950, we were even further away from medical help. The nearest doctors were in Bairnsdale or in Wangaratta. Fortunately, for the one occasion at Glen Valley where my family needed help, a new family had recently moved to live there. The young wife had not so long ago completed her training as a nurse at St Vincent's Hospital in Fitzroy in Melbourne. This was the first time that I had heard of St Vincent's Hospital but the second time that I had heard of Fitzroy.

In 1951 when we moved yet again, now to Yarrambat on the outskirts of Melbourne, we were a little closer to two medical practices. The nearer one was run by Dr Don Cordner in Diamond Creek while his brother, Dr Ted Cordner, ran a practice in Greensborough. Dr Don Cordner made a home visit to examine me when I refused to attend High School one day because of belly pain. He excluded appendicitis much to my mother's relief.

My only other interactions with doctors came at boarding school, once for an injection of penicillin for a large boil on my forehead and once for sutures for a football-related cut above my right eye. Thus, there were few interactions with the medical profession that might explain my career choice.

In 1952 I did attend a dentist in Greensborough on more than one occasion because of dental decay and the need for fillings. These were not pleasant experiences. His drill was low speed as was the case then for all dentists. The chain that drove the drill had attached to it images of a train and these images, immediately in front of the young patient, were meant to distract one from the discomfort of the drilling. They failed. It was only some years later when the high-speed drill was introduced that my dislike of seeing the dentist faded.

11

Deeper and Higher into the Australian Bush

In January 1950, a large furniture van, paid for by the Education Department, arrived at Freeburgh to take our belongings to our new home at Glen Valley, a small township situated high in the Australian Alps about twenty-five miles north west of Omeo.

Packing up for our move was fun for me as we were encouraged to help in the task. While we did not have a lot of possessions, in the process of packing, one was likely to find possessions that had been long forgotten. We did not have access to large cardboard boxes for packing but instead were given a number of wooden crates by our neighbour, the Greek orchardist. These were normally used for dispatching his apples to the market.

The furniture van was the largest truck that I had ever seen. I did not get to ride in it but my father and our dog Nip fitted easily into its large cabin alongside the driver and his assistant. Everything on board, our bicycles loaded last, off they went. My mother, I and my younger sister travelled separately and arrived a day later. My older brother and sister were already in Melbourne where they were to board with relatives and so continue their secondary education. My father later enjoyed recounting the journey over two mountain passes in a truck with faulty brakes.

For our journey, we went by bus to Wangaratta and then took a second bus to Mitta Mitta, a town nestled on the western slopes of the Alps. Here we stayed overnight at the only hotel. That night for our dinner we were served pink cabbage; our mother explained that cabbage turned pink if it was over-cooked. Next morning the bus took us up an unsealed narrow mountainous road, almost to the summit of Mt Wills at 5200 feet (1584 metres) and then down the other side past Sunnyside and Glen Wills to our destination, Glen Valley, two to three kilometres south east of Glen Wills. The bus then went on to Omeo. In 1950, Sunnyside was a ghost town and Glen Wills almost so.

My father had been sent to Glen Valley as the headmaster and sole teacher at this small school. I have undertaken little research but I confidently claim that, at that time, Glen Valley, at around 4000 feet above sea-level, was the most elevated and isolated town in Victoria.

Glen Valley could be accessed from Melbourne by train to Wangaratta and then by bus as we had done. It could also be accessed by train to Bairnsdale, bus to Omeo, and then a second bus from Omeo for the trip to Glen Valley. Either way, by public transport the journey took two days. The narrow highway from Omeo was unsealed and it traversed rugged mountainous country with some precipitous drops on the side of the road in places.

The township of Glen Valley is now just a spot on the map but in 1950 it had a single room primary school with an attendance of around thirty pupils. Like Freeburgh, Glen Valley owed its existence to the Victorian gold rush. Gold was first discovered on the slopes of nearby Mt Wills in the early 1890s. By 1894 the population of Glen Wills had reached 500 and by 1910 Glen Wills and its surrounding mining area had a population of around 7000 people, many of whom were gold prospectors living in tents. In 1950 there was a single gold mine still operating at Glen Valley and there were a few small farms in the district. There were four or five houses in the valley within walking distance of the school. We lived in one of these.

The Glen Valley school in 1950

The only shop in Glen Valley was a small general store situated opposite our house beside the narrow unsealed highway. The general store also served as the post office. The post office had the only telephone in the district. The school was a further 500 metres up the road towards Glen Wills. There was a hotel but this was at Glen Wills, a further two to three kilometres past the school. Apart from the hotel, Glen Wills was a ghost town and the hotel was the last reminder of the gold rush era.

One way of learning of the 'life-cycle' of the gold rush towns of Victoria is to view the records of when any such town was first allocated a post office and when the post office was closed. For Glen Wills the years were from 1890 until 1936 and for Glen Valley from

1908 until 1973. The Freeburgh post office had lasted longer – from 1869 to 1969.

Close to the Glen Valley school was a tiny timber one room shop which hosted the butcher from Omeo when he visited for one day each week. The building was otherwise not in use. Supplies, newspapers and mail came via the bus that ran from Omeo via Glen Valley and Mitta Mitta to Wangaratta each day. My recollection is that the bus ran in one direction one day and did the return trip two days later; this is consistent with our overnight stay at Mitta Mitta. Our newspapers were always two days old. Our radio did not function well at Glen Valley so we were indeed isolated. For medical help, the nearest doctors were in Bairnsdale and Wangaratta.

My father was an avid reader of newspapers all his life, usually subscribing to all the major Melbourne dailies which in the 1950s included the *Age*, the *Argus* and the *Sun News Pictorial*. The *Argus* had a section for younger readers in which I took an interest. Each week the editor of the junior section identified a topic for debate and readers were invited to contribute. One week while we were living at Glen Valley, the debating topic was on city life versus country life. I sent in a contribution and to my great thrill it was accepted. It was my first publication. This is what was published in the *Argus* on 24th of November in 1950:

Country Life

I think country life is better. At any rate, you can go on long walks in the country without getting killed. In the city you can't go for walks without danger of being killed. It's better living in the country, and going to the city for your holidays. By going to school in the country you can have more fun than going to school in the city. Think of the fun you can have going looking for birds' nests in the country.

Kerry Breen, Glen Valley, via Omeo

The house we lived in was not owned by the Education Department. It was even more basic than the house at Freeburgh as it was weatherboard and had never been painted. We again relied on tank water. For lighting we at first used our kerosene lamps but then my parents purchased a Tilley brand pressure lantern from the general store. I was astounded at how bright this light was when compared to our kerosene lamps.

Our daily lives at Glen Valley differed little from Freeburgh. My mother no longer had to milk our cow. Instead, we depended on powdered milk or condensed milk that came in sealed cans. The biggest difference in our lives came with the one winter that we spent there. It was generally much colder than Freeburgh and it often snowed heavily. There were many days when access from Mitta Mitta was not possible because the road was closed by snow at Mt Wills.

We walked to school in the snow wearing gum boots. By now I was capable of using a saw and a hammer so I built a rough toboggan that worked in a fashion. We built snowmen and had snowball fights in the school ground. My strongest memory of the impact of snow on the environment comes from a day (not a school day) when I was permitted to walk on my own to Glen Wills and beyond. Six inches of snow had fallen overnight and the views of the snow-covered valley were breathtakingly beautiful. In addition, the snow seemed to buffer or reduce the usual sounds of life and everything seemed hushed. On that walk I came across some kangaroos and also a 'family' of emus walking through snow-covered open grassland. On another walk, when it had not snowed, I had the rare privilege of sighting a lyrebird at close quarters.

The cold winter weather had other impacts. We had to be careful to leave the kitchen tap gently dripping overnight. If we did not, there was a risk that the water in the pipe that led from our rain tank would freeze and, via its expansion, burst the pipe. Our house was so cold that my sister and I would not get out of bed until our mother had lit the kitchen stove. Then we would dress beside the warm stove. Our father had his own story of the indoor cold. He recounted that one morning his shaving lather froze on his face. This is probably true as our thermometer recorded the temperature indoors that morning at 18 degrees Fahrenheit (freezing point is 32 degrees Fahrenheit). The school had a large slow combustion heater and, together with the large number of pupils in the single classroom, we were kept warm.

With the larger school numbers, my mother worked part-time as a teacher's aide at the school. Our house was close enough that in lunch hour we would often walk home for lunch. We also walked home with her after school. One day I challenged her to race me home. She finished well ahead of me; that was when I learnt that she used to compete with the Essendon Harriers athletic club after she left school.

It was at Glen Valley that I first participated in the ball game of 'Up and de over'. With thirty children we had two large teams to compete and the game could go on for a long time. It may well be that this game was invented at Glen Valley – or perhaps an earlier teacher introduced it. We all were expected to practise team games for the forthcoming interschool sports day. These included tunnel ball and some other games. These sessions, supervised by my father, were in class time set aside for physical education.

In late spring of 1950, all the Glen Valley school pupils travelled to the district sports carnival held that year at Swifts Creek which is 26 km south of Omeo. To get there, most of the students rode in the empty tray of a tip-truck borrowed for the day from the local gold mine. I have little memory of the day other than that we all took rugs or blankets to sit on and to keep us warm during the trip home late in the evening. On the way there we stopped to stretch our legs at the Blue Duck Inn which is situated halfway between Glen Valley and Omeo. Here my father took a group photo with his Brownie box camera. Having driven these mountain roads as an adult, I have often had cause to reflect on the enormous responsibility placed on the truck driver to get us safely to Swifts Creek and back.

Glen Valley school children outside the Blue Duck Inn, 1950

Nearby to our house in Glen Valley, a farmer had created three holes for golf. The grass of his fairways was kept short by his sheep. His greens were made of sand, called 'sand scrapes' in golfing parlance. You were allowed to rake the surface smooth before you putted. My father owned three or four ancient golf clubs with wooden shafts and we played there a couple of times.

In the summer there was little opportunity to go swimming. The nearest river (called locally the Big River but really the upper reach of the Mitta River) was a four mile walk to get to. I can only recall one trip to swim in it.

I have earlier described the tennis tournament that my father organised for the folks of Glen Valley. The other sport that I was enthusiastic about was Australian football. I was raised to barrack for Essendon and my interest grew rapidly when in 1949 a football 'freak' named John Coleman made his debut for the team. At Glen Valley in fourth grade I soon made friends with a boy in my grade. He lived close to the school and the tennis court and we spent much time together playing sport. He was more talented at sport but I did a little better in school work.

In football he barracked for Carlton. We were both keen to own a football jumper in our team's colours and we prevailed on our parents to place a mail order at about the same time. Soon we were kicking a football back and forth to each other, he in a Carlton jumper and me in my Essendon jumper on which my mother had sewn Coleman's number, number 10. (It was at Glen Valley that my attempt to knit a pair of football socks in Essendon colours was not very successful.) After we left Glen Valley I did not keep in touch with this friend but recently found him in Omeo. He finished high school at Omeo and then built a career around his natural talent as a painter of landscapes and as a draughtsman. He and his wife now run an art gallery in Omeo. He told me that during the time that his family lived at Glen Valley, his father was the local 'SP bookie'.

When the summer school holidays arrived in late December 1950 we were looking forward to a planned holiday with Grandma Breen in Essendon, but this did not eventuate. My older brother and sister first came home for Christmas. They came via Bairnsdale and stayed one night in a hotel in Omeo before taking the bus to Glen Valley. Unfortunately, they brought the measles with them. All we four children came down with measles seriatim so there was no holiday at Essendon.

My older sister was very ill with high temperatures and at times was delirious. She may well have had measles encephalitis. Fortunately, earlier that year, our new neighbours, Adrian and Pat Black had arrived in Glen Valley. Pat had not so long ago finished her nursing training at St Vincent's Hospital in Melbourne and she came to help my mother care for my sister. She stayed overnight for three or four nights, leaving Adrian to care for their baby Tony. This generous assistance bound our families for the rest of our lives. My mother and Pat remained firm friends when both families moved back to Melbourne. I attended Pat's 80th birthday celebration and sadly also her funeral ten years or so later. I am still in regular contact with some of her children.

My sister made a full recovery from measles and, with my older brother, returned to Melbourne for the start of the school year. Meanwhile the rest of the family looked forward to another year in Glen Valley but this was not to be.

Each month in the mail, my father received his copy of the latest gazette published by the Victorian Education Department. He encouraged me as a nine-year old to peruse it. A large section listed teaching vacancies around the state. Each vacancy was categorised as being open to teachers of a certain classification. That classification was based on years of experience and the rating of the school inspectors. The listing also indicated whether the position came with a teacher's residence. I enjoyed the task, partly because, like my father, I was keen to get closer to Melbourne and partly because I was learning where in Victoria these various country towns were located.

A school at Yarrambat met my father's classification and the wish to be closer to Melbourne. The school also came with a teacher's residence. His application was successful and as result we departed Glen Valley in the May school holidays of 1951. We moved into the teacher's residence at Yarrambat just before the start of the second term of 1951. Within a couple of months, a remarkable event happened. It snowed heavily at Yarrambat for the first time in fifty years and several centimetres of snow lay on the ground for a day or so.

12

Closer to Melbourne but still at a Bush School

Anyone who visits the outer Melbourne suburb of Yarrambat nowadays is entitled to be sceptical of my description of the Yarrambat Primary School in 1951 as a bush school – but a typical bush school it certainly was. Yarrambat then was primarily a farming district although there had been some gold mines in the district, the most recent having been sunk in 1939.

The town's centre was a collection of four buildings: the single room primary school and its adjacent teacher's residence, a small general store/post office which was diagonally across Ironbark Road from the school, and the Yarrambat community hall 200 metres further down Ironbark Road, towards the town of Diamond Creek. Otherwise, there were very few houses within a kilometre of the school. Diamond Creek was an hour's walk away. This was where the nearest hotel stood, and where the nearest doctor, Dr Donald Cordner, practised.

The Yarrambat School accommodated all six grades in a single large classroom, typical of a bush school. As there was a bus that took older children to a high school in Eltham, the primary school teacher at Yarrambat was not required to teach Grades 7 and 8.

Snow-covered Yarrambat School, July 1951

In one sense, my 'bush' childhood ended when we moved to Yarrambat as now we could readily take a bus and train into Melbourne. I even travelled with my family to Essendon one day in 1954 to see our new Queen Elizabeth arriving to visit her loyal subjects. Relatives living in Melbourne often visited us at weekends and my cousin Gary Breen who was my age came to stay with us on a couple of occasions. We at last had good radio reception. This enhanced reception of several Melbourne radio stations provided my young mind with a puzzle: how could the same singer be in two radio stations at the same time? We had never owned a record player so I had no knowledge of the use of recorded music.

However, many other facets of daily life remained the same as if we were still living in the more remote bush. We had no electricity, telephone, sewerage, septic tank or night-cart service. We relied on rain water collected in our one tank. We still had our bath on Sunday night with water warmed by a Mallee chip heater. At the nearby post office there was a red telephone box with a coin-operated telephone. My father quickly reactivated a large area of the school grounds that had been a vegetable garden. A local farmer sold us a 'billy can' of fresh unpasteurised milk every day: it was often my task to walk the kilometre and back for the milk. We were still using a wood stove, kerosene lamps and bedside candles. Our Coolgardie safe was soon replaced by a second-hand kerosene-powered refrigerator. This was surprisingly efficient. To celebrate its arrival, my mother made ice cream using the recipe on a can of Carnation brand ('from contented cows') sweetened condensed milk.

My father must have pestered the Public Works Department via the Education Department repeatedly while we lived at Yarrambat. A short history of the school, published for its centenary in 1978, reported that in 1951 the then headmaster, M L Breen, had written to the Department to say that the teacher's residence was in a dilapidated state as it had been unoccupied for some years. Seeing this record surprised me as our new home was little different from our homes in Freeburgh and Glen Valley. His pestering had at least two effects. While we lived there, the house was repainted and a rotary Hills clothes hoist (an Australian invention) was installed in our back yard.

In that backyard were also a hen house, a large open shed or garage and, of course, in the back corner, our outdoor 'dunny'. We had little use for the shed so it became a large doll's house for my younger sister. I soon took over the running of the hen house. This was the result of a program at the Yarrambat school called the 'Young Farmer's Club'. I assume that the program was an effort on the part of the Education Department to engage young rural minds in what was involved in running a successful farm. My younger sister and I were the only pupils at the school who were not living on a farm and thus running our hen house became my 'Young Farmer's' project.

The front gate to the teacher's residence at Yarrambat

This proved to be educational. My mother took me to buy some newly hatched chickens and later we bought a rooster so soon I was hatching my own chickens. In an exercise book, I kept a daily record of egg production. I observed that if my hens were fed shell grit (ground sea shells) their egg shells were much stronger. I also observed that if my hens were allowed to roam free in our back yard and graze on the fresh grass, the yolks of their eggs became a deeper shade of yellow. I contributed some of my hens' eggs to the annual Lord Mayor of Melbourne Egg Appeal, designed to raise money for the city's public hospitals. This appeal operated via the schools and schools competed to be recognised as the largest donor.

My hen house at Yarrambat

While there were many aspects of life at Yarrambat that were congenial, I do not have warm memories of my school experience. I think that there were two connected reasons for this. For the first time I was forced to come to terms with the reality that the school teacher was also my father. I had become so used to addressing him as 'Sir' at school and reverting to 'Dad' at home that it never occurred to me that this might cause me grief. At Yarrambat it did. I still don't know why. There was a boy a year ahead of me who was a bully. His attitude may have been influenced by a disability in that he had a limp – perhaps as a result of polio. I was hounded by him and his acolytes as a 'teacher's pet'. This situation may have been aggravated by my father's approach to the issue. In order to avoid this accusation, he was tough on me and when I did well, the hounding only increased. I dared not complain to him so I suffered in silence.

Once again there was the district school sports day to prepare for. In 1952 when I was in Grade 6, the event was held at Whittlesea. On this occasion most of the children were transported in the back of a high-sided truck provided by a local farmer. The families of Yarrambat were a little better off than at Glen Valley so we nearly all wore white tops, white shorts, white socks and white sand shoes. To be identified in any event, we added one of the limited supply of the coloured sashes to our outfit. The Yarrambat sash colour was pink.

Off to the interschool sports, 1952; my parents standing beside the farmer's truck

In preparation for the day, my father arranged 'try outs' for individual events. I thought that I was a fast sprinter but he had me race a new boy who turned out to be faster! At the time, I blamed my father for my defeat. To find a flat space for 100 yards, he took the two of us to an area just beyond the community hall. It was very grassy and the grass was slippery. I wanted to race in my football boots to get a better grip – but the headmaster would not permit it! Later at a larger school, it became apparent that I was not a particularly fast runner.

At Yarrambat we introduced 'Up and de over' and the game was played with enthusiasm. For the two winters at that school, the favourite pastime at recess was skipping. One took turns at either end of the long rope: any time you failed to jump the rope, you took over the turning of it. Hopscotch was also popular. I can't recall playing football with other students but when school was out, the large school ground was the place where my brother and I played 'kick to kick' endlessly.

My father encouraged his pupils to enter various children's handiwork competitions at the annual agricultural show at Whittlesea. I opted for the woodwork competition. We owned basic carpentry tools including a saw, a chisel, a screw driver and a hammer, but not much more. I had taught myself in a fashion as I was the child who would help my mother if something around the house needed fixing. My mother knew quite a lot about carpentry as her father had been a carpenter and her younger brother had followed in the same trade. Nevertheless, I cannot recall that she ever instructed me.

In the first year, 1952, that I entered the competition I created a simple relief image of the footballer John Coleman on a rectangle of soft timber measuring approximately 12 cm by 18 cm. I traced a photo of Coleman taken from a daily newspaper and coloured the image in red and black for his guernsey and socks and white for his shorts. To create the relief effect, I chiselled away fragments of wood or hammered parts of the soft timber flatter with an upturned nail. To my surprise I was awarded first prize (for my age group).

The woodwork and the prize certificate

I was now committed to the competition. I managed to find a couple of large wooden boxes made of soft wood. I seem to recall that these were used for shipping ammunition for shotguns. Each box had a lid made of a single piece of the same timber. The timber was very easy to work with. So the next year my entry was a first aid box, with a shelf inside and a hinged door. I painted the entire box white and added a large red cross painted on the door. In the process of painting, I learnt something else about this very soft timber – the timber soaked up my paint and it took several coats to achieve the effect that I was seeking. That effort also won me first prize as did a shoe box made out of the same type of wood the following year.

Like most boys of my age, I was keen to own a billycart. We could not afford to buy one so I scrounged around for suitable materials. Four wheels came from an old pram and the ubiquitous kerosene tin helped to make a bonnet for the cart. The most difficult aspect was designing and building the front axle such that one could steer the cart with two ropes tied to the axle. I painted the billycart in 'British racing green' and gave it the number 7. A photo shows the completed product. There were only gravel roads in the area so I never had the pleasure of seeking to coast in it down a hill on a surfaced road.

The billycart with my younger sister at the 'wheel'

99

Within the school grounds there was a tennis court with a surface of white clay. It had seen better days, its surrounding fence was in disarray, and a third of the court was overgrown with couch grass. The net was gone but there were still the posts and a wire (the remains of a net) strung between them. We Breen children managed to clear away the couch grass. We found that there were still pegs in the ground that marked the dimensions of the court. By pulling a piece of string tightly between the relevant pegs, we could scratch lines in the clay and now were able to play tennis on the court.

With an interest in tennis, I was permitted to travel on my own by bus and train to Kooyong for two days of the Australian Open. This would have been in January 1954 when I was thirteen. I must have become bored with the tennis as I spent some time with a boy my age collecting empty drink bottles for pocket money. I learnt a valuable lesson. At the end of the first day, my new friend asked if I could lend him four shillings, which I did. He said that he would meet me at that same spot the following day to repay me. I never saw him again!

Rabbits were as prevalent at Yarrambat as they had been at Freeburgh but we did not hunt them so often. Our dog Nip was now older and overweight. She could find the rabbits but she could not catch any. A farmer neighbour who as a hobby bred greyhounds for racing sold us a greyhound for £5.00. She was a beautiful calm dog who fitted into our family immediately. We named her Bambi. With her we now could go rabbiting again. Nip would sniff out a rabbit and Bambi would catch it. This sport did not last long as the myxomatosis virus had been released in 1950 and by 1952 the virus had reached Yarrambat; many of the rabbits we saw were ill and dying.

Our dog Nip at Yarrambat with my older brother

Our school yard fence and the front gate to our house were not fully dog proof and we had failed to train Bambi not to go out on to Ironbark Road. One day a distressed motorist knocked on our door to tell us that Bambi had run into the path of his car and was dead. We buried her in the backyard.

As at every other school in which my father taught, he arranged an end of year school concert held in the local hall. I can only recall my participation in Grade Six. That year he encouraged me to learn a poem by heart to recite at the concert. I managed to do that and recited it without missing a beat. In reading the poem again as an adult I am surprised how long it is. He had selected the Australian bush ballad of Thomas Spencer (1845–1911) entitled '*How MacDougall Topped the Score*'. His choice was undoubtedly based on its opening line which reads 'A peaceful spot is Piper's Flat'. My version was altered to begin with 'A peaceful spot is Yarrambat'. It is an amusing tale, worth reading and easily found on the internet.

Swimming in summer time was restricted by the distance we had to walk through a farmer's paddocks to reach the Plenty River. At Yarrambat the river was at the bottom of a deep gorge down which we clambered. One summer, the Yarrambat community arranged a picnic day at the beach. The chosen beach was Seaford on Port Phillip Bay, a 70 km trip. The transport for this event was a furniture van. In the back of the large van were three long backless bench seats, not fixed down in any way. The back of the van was left open. This was a common mode of transport then. It was much cheaper than hiring a bus and the van operators were happy because nobody moved house on a Sunday. My other memory of this day, which was only my second visit to the sea, was how much more buoyant was the salt water when compared to river water.

In summer, in all three places of my childhood there was always a risk of bushfire. We did not experience any fires near our house at Freeburgh or Glen Valley. In 1939, two years ahead of our arrival at Freeburgh, the disastrous fires of that summer destroyed the fence around the Freeburgh School. At Yarrambat a grass fire broke out one summer on the side of a road not far beyond the community hall. Locals rushed to put it out, including local school children. I went to help, lacking any safety clothing. I was given a hessian sack to beat the fire out. Luckily the fire had been detected early and was soon put out.

One other memorable community event that took place was a children's fancy dress competition and ball at the Yarrambat Hall. My younger sister and I cajoled our mother into creating a fancy dress costume for each of us. For my sister, my mother made a traditional Dutch national costume dress which was complex and very attractive. It went over my young head that her choice was almost certainly connected with her Dutch heritage. Her paternal grandfather was Dutch. As a young seaman, he jumped ship in Melbourne and stayed. My request for my mother was for me to attend in a Superman costume. Again, my inventive and resourceful mother met this challenge. She put a lot of time and effort into the two costumes and she must have been disappointed that neither costume won a prize.

My mother's creative work

We lived at Yarrambat for three and a half years. I completed Grade Six at the end of 1952 so for the last two years at Yarrambat, I took the school bus every day to the Eltham High School. The bus ran down Yan Yean Road past Doreen, Yarrambat and Plenty to Greensborough and then via Briar Hill and Montmorency to Eltham.

The Yarrambat contingent was among the first to get on to the bus and last to get off in the evening. The bus picked up two boys at Plenty and it was several months until I became aware that these two boys were living at a large orphanage.

Eltham was definitely not part of the bush so my 'bush' childhood ended when I started at high school. For my younger sister, this was not the case. In December 1954, the Education Department directed my father to move to Greenvale, yet again a single room, one teacher school in what was then a rural area much like Yarrambat. Because of difficulty of public transport, when we moved to Greenvale, I was sent to a country boarding school for my last four years of high school. By going to boarding school, I did not get all the benefits from the modern amenities of the teacher's residence that had only recently been constructed in the grounds of the Greenvale Primary School. Of special note was an indoor toilet connected to a septic tank. Almost as important was the capacity to turn on a bright electric light in every room with the flick of a switch! With electricity came running hot water. The real bush was now a long way away.

The newly-built teacher's residence at Greenvale, 1955

Epilogue

In this description of a childhood in the Australian bush, I have deliberately focussed on how people lived from the perspective of the physical environment and its associated limited amenities for daily living. I have left it to the reader to try to imagine the social and psychological impacts the environment might have had on the lives of those living in the bush. At my tender years, I could not have had any useful insights in to those impacts at the time anyhow.

I have also sought to record for posterity how bush schools functioned and what demands were placed on bush school teachers in that era.

I have pondered from time to time as an adult in what ways my personal development and approach to life may have been influenced by living my first twelve years in the bush. Any influences are of course difficult to untangle for, no matter where I lived, I would have still been raised by a school teacher father and a mother who later became a teacher herself.

Only two aspects clearly stand out for me. The lack of access to children's books hastened my development as a reader and stimulated my love of books and of writing. Second, long after I moved to live an urban life, I found that in making new friends I automatically identified with those who had also been raised in the bush.

My choice of career was unrelated to my childhood experiences and was probably a happy accident. However as a doctor I found that

I could relate readily to the many patients I encountered who came from rural areas and I also found that I had great empathy for, and could communicate easily with, people who were not well off, whether from the bush or the city.

Appendix

Autobiography of Leo Breen (1907–1983)

(Incomplete, written circa 1980–83; it was hand-written and has since been typed without any editing. The explanatory footnotes were added at the time of typing.)

Summary

Born Kooreh* 17-7-1907. Uncertain of my recollections of infancy there. Do I really remember being down in the cellar during the bushfire which destroyed the whole farm except for the house? Do I remember that my mother, in a last desperate throw, hung holy pictures on the outside wall? Before my reaching school age, my father took over my grandfather's farm at Sutherland. (Kooreh is in the hilly country south of St Arnaud, Sutherland is north of St Arnaud, each about six miles out; it was at Sutherland where the plains, the wheat country, began.)

My first clear recollection of Sutherland is my first day at school when I was put on the Shetland pony, Sailor, led by my big brother Jim, and wept all the way. I'll return to the Sutherland school here and there during 'my tale of sound and fury, told by an idiot, signifying nothing'.

---

* Kooreh was the name of the family farm near St Arnaud.

When I was twelve years old the farm that my grandfather had built up very successfully was sold and a general store at Kilmore was purchased. I spent four years there as a student at Assumption College. Much more later we for a few weeks we lived, some of us, in rooms above a 'delicatessen' in Victoria St, Brunswick, near the railway station. I made an application to the Victorian Education Department for a position as junior teacher and also answered an advertisement for a lad (I was sixteen) to work for a small firm of heliographers in Collins St, Melbourne. I enjoyed lunch time very much, my first taste of 'Saturday Evening Post' which ran a serial about a Wodehouse manservant named Psmith. What Jeeves addict has ever heard of Psmith. More later.

In May of that year, 1924, I was appointed as junior teacher at Glenroy. I now list, in case time runs short, my teaching appointments:

1928   Melbourne Teachers College

1929   Head teacher, with part-time assistant, at Arawata near Korumburra

1931   After several months of illness (multiple infective arthritis*) spent two terms as an assistant teacher at Geelong Rd, Footscray.

---

* Leo spent 5-6 months in the old Melbourne Hospital in Lonsdale St. Multiple infective arthritis would now be called 'post-infective reactive arthritis' and in genetically disposed people is a harbinger of ankylosing spondylitis, which eventually severely restricted Leo and also affected his brother Vincent and Vin's twin sister Florence.

1931   In September I was appointed H.T*. at Coromby just six miles out of Murtoa. As I stepped out of the train I felt I was back again at Sutherland some forty-five miles to the east. A few clumps of buloke and box-trees and long, long miles of green wheat.

1936   Moved to Lubeck School, fourteen miles to the south-east, to save fifteen shillings in week rent. This was a mistake, one of many.

1938   Moved to Ocean Grove, again as Head Teacher. This was another more serious mistake. There was no school residence at O G and the weekend houses proved inadequate.

1941   Moved to Freeburgh, near Bright, mainly to get back in a school residence.

1949/50 Appointed H.T. at Glen Valley†.

1951   Applied for and obtained H.T. position at Yarrambat, six miles from Greensborough and 3 and 1/2 miles from Diamond Creek.

1955   After a brief period as H.T. at Greenvale, 5 miles from Essendon, put in for promotion and thereafter positions as assistant teacher at Kensington and finally at Glenroy West. My happiest years as a teacher were at Arawata, amongst the Methodist-Presbyterian dairy farmers and graziers, at Coromby among the Lutheran wheat farmers and at Glenroy West, where there were many fine people with splendid children.

* Head teacher.
† Glen Valley is a tiny hamlet north west of Omeo.

Chapter 1 – Intransigence

Yes, I know that 'intransigence' is a word used by very intelligent people like Mr R J Hawke. In fact, I have used it of Mr H himself. A few years ago some member of my family bought a camera from the A.C.T.U.'s store in Melbourne as a present for another member of my family. But member no.2 already had very good camera but found herself unable to get it exchanged for some other article. When she received a letter curtly informing her that no exchanging or refund was possible, I took over and wrote to the arrogant, ill-mannered woman, expressing regret that Mr Hawke's bright future would not be enhanced or advanced by the 'intransigence' of his business associates.

However, I now realise that intransigence has been the very stuff of my life. In hindsight it first appeared clearly when as a junior teacher at Glenroy I questioned the very conservative political opinions of the very capable headmaster, Mr Thomas G. Strange, who was instructing a Miss A. M. Warren in the strange world of politics. Miss Warren, perhaps the best primary teacher I have ever met, suggested to me later that as I was seventeen or eighteen a little young to argue with Mr S.

I was at that time, quite successfully getting rid of an inferiority complex, that's what the experts called it fifty years ago, about speaking in public. I had joined a very old mate, Herb McIvor, probably about this year.

The first clear indication of my tendency to be critical of constituted authority occurred in the first four weeks of my year at Melbourne Teachers College. In those days, the primary students, the secondary, the manual arts and, perhaps, the infant teacher students were all part of the same establishment. The scholarly Professor Wrigley, who probably wrote much more convincingly than he spoke, was Principal. I don't remember that he took any 'prime' lectures and it must have been at the weekly assembly that I heard him say 'Tennyrate' over and over again. Though not as often as Malcolm Fraser says 'you know' or 'look'. Both are the last resort of the illiterate and inarticulate. I know that Douglas Wilkie of the 'Sun News Pictorial', the King Street Bridge backwater equivalent of the Nashville 'Banner' plucks absurd lies about Russia off the top of his head but his award of M.A (Oxon) to the lad from Tangamalangoloo still has me puzzled. If you want to know why I call Tamie's dear Malcolm the lad from T., you'll have to read John O'Brien's 'Around the Boree Log'. Of course it may be included in...

Mr G. S. Browne, the Vice-Principal, and head of the primary section, was quite a contrast to Professor W. It is not true to say that he was 'all show'. I still think he was an excellent lecturer. In early 1928 he arranged a Parliamentary debate, open to all students, on a Saturday night at Melbourne Teachers College. The subject was 'In modern society are people really free?' or something like that. Though this was not quite the clear-cut question debated in C.Y.M.S. competition, I welcomed the freedom such a theme and the whole concept of a Parliamentary debate gave to an A grade C.Y.M.S. debater. I received an early call and began, in quite un-C.Y.M.S. fashion by reciting my record of interviews with people in the street. The Speaker, G.S. Browne (Greasy) himself, endured this until I came to the girl at Flinders Street Railway Station selling orange drink tickets. When I asked her 'Are you free?', G. S. Browne, later Professor of Education, intervened and asked me to confine myself to the subject of the debate. In 1928 I was not sufficiently articulate to say: 'for Chrisake, I am on the subject' and merely protested quite forcibly that I was taking part in a Parliamentary debate and claimed the right to develop my argument in any way I pleased. I completed my submission in a straight C.Y.M.S. fashion but could not resist a final dig at G.S. 'you have seen in the past few minutes that Melbourne Teachers' College students are certainly not free'.

Our first period on Monday morning was 'Psychology' (I still prefer William James) taken by that extremely competent lecturer, G.S. Browne. Announcing the subject of this particular session, he made reference to his last lecture and then shocked me out of my Monday morning coma by saying 'Would Mr Breen please tell us what a reflex action is?' I was dumbfounded, couldn't think, taken by surprise, plain buggered, when Tom Cole behind me whispered 'sneezing'. I replied 'One example, sir, is sneezing'.

So far, so good, but I didn't realise that I was to suffer, at the end of the year, from my refusal to accept dictation. I have only now, more than fifty years later, appreciated that even (especially?) academics can be mean-minded little men. Read C.P Snow. 'Ectually' as Professor Wrigley used to say, I had great respect for G.S. Browne. I thought he was, apart from the mellifluous, eloquent Dr Daniel Mannix, the best speaker I had ever heard. So much so, that during that year, in the C.Y.M.S. open oration contest at North Melbourne Town Hall, I adopted one of his mannerisms and thereby lost the contest. The only criticism the adjudicator had of me was that, instead of using both hands for gestures and gesticulation, I usually kept one hand in my coat pocket. G.S. had a brown double-breaster and he had a habit, when lecturing, of keeping his right hand in his coat pocket. I also had a double-breasted suit, navy blue, tailor-made by Mr H.G. Bridge of Essendon. I am not sure now whether I paid him five shillings a fortnight or two shillings and sixpence a fortnight. That was my Sunday suit and I don't ever remember wearing it to Melbourne Teachers College. My uniform was a pair of grey slacks and a really good quality hand-me-down sports coat that had belonged to my oldest brother, Jim. Clothes can be so important. I completed the year at Melbourne Teachers College with high marks in all subjects and with five or six others and 'outstanding' mark in teaching but instead of finishing in the first half dozen as some of my friends had predicted, I was seventeenth of 130. No list was posted showing our marks, including 'social participation'. My social participation approached excellent standards. I attended every Saturday night dance, I played football, tennis, badminton and led my House debating team. However I had no intention of accepting a second year studentship; I wanted the 226 pounds a year that went with the management of a rural school.

Chapter 2 – Animals I have known

Up at Glen Valley about 1951, I found myself in a quandary or perhaps the horns of a dilemma. Actually it was at Glen Wills that I found myself perplexed. I'll try to explain. The gold mine known as the Maude and Yellow Girl had started in the nineties at Sunnyside and worked down, underground, three miles to Glen Wills and then another mile and a half to Glen Valley. When I arrived in 1951, somewhat unwillingly, to take charge of the school at Glen Valley, the pub was at Glen Wills but the Post Office, store, mine and most of the residents were at Glen Valley.

Being rather fond of the grog, I developed a habit of walking up to the pub after school on Friday. An occasional visit on Saturday was a bonus. On this Friday evening I had to decide what to back in the Caulfield Cup to be run next day. That's right, Saturday. I had two fancies, the favourite, Grey Boots, and a fairly successful handicapper, Carapooee.

I never put my two-bob on a favourite but this time I had a sentimental reason for backing Grey Boots. Though I had been born at Kooreh, south of St Arnaud, Victoria, Australia, I spent all my primary school years, from the age of six to twelve, on a wheat farm six miles to the north of St Arnaud (see Chapter 5, 'The Holy Picture on the Wall'). At Sutherland, we had several hacks and I don't mean party hacks. These were horses that we rode or drove in the buggy or the gig.

My favourite horse was a grey pony we called Boots. The bootmaker we bought him from, all right, all right, from whom we bought him, called him Jack, but as that was my father's name, my mother did not think the name suitable. So he was named Boots. And what a prize he turned out to be. He was a beautiful hack and could amble like a dream – you know ambling? It's a sort of half walk, half canter, a rhythmic form of equestrian progress. I'd like to see Bill Roycroft on a good ambler. That was a wonderful performance in Rome, Mr Roycroft. As a great Australian, I rank you with Ben Chifley, Doc Evatt, John Curtin and Dr Jim Cairns. As boys we thought Australian horsemen were the best in the world and suddenly you and your team proved that we were right.

Boots was such a good ambler that at a sports meeting in Feeney's paddock at Swanwater in 1919, in aid of Sutherland school funds, I managed to persuade my father to let me ride Boots in the walk, trot and gallop. After all, my older brothers, Jim and Jack had ridden in the previous events, Jim on Ladybird in a hunter's contest and Jack on Gerry (Jerry) in the hack race. My idea, a twelve year old misconception, was that Boots, ambling, would get such a lead in the walk that he could hold it in the trot and the gallop.

When we lined up, me on the outside of fifteen big men on fifteen big horses, my withdrawal, taking some thirty years, from the Catholic Church began. Father Manning, a priest for whom I had developed a great respect because largely of his quail-shooting ability, was the starter. When he announced that amblers would be disqualified, I was shrivelled. I held Boots down to a walk until I realised that the big horses, well ahead, were ambling away to their hearts' content. I finished second last only because Mr Hancock was pulling his mount up. My school mates were quite hilarious. I did, however, save face by winning the Siamese race – three-legged they call it now – with Jack H.

Boots was a first-class stock-horse. He could turn on a sixpence and knew before his rider, speaking for myself, what the horses, cattle or sheep he was rounding up were likely to do. Of course, he had his faults. He was often hard to catch, so much so that he was sometimes subjected to the indignity of being half-hobbled, i.e. had a chain strapped to his off fore-leg. 'Off' in horsemen's parlance means right, 'near' is left. So the driver of a team, when he wants to turn right, cries 'Gee off' and I was almost septuagenarian before I realised that when he wished the horses to turn left, he called 'Come near'; I always thought it was 'Come in here'.

I had always known that, when catching a horse, you did not approach from the rear unless you wanted a kick on the chin. But once, after school, when all the other pupils had gone home, I forgot that cardinal precept. In the pony paddock I found Boots in one of his niggly, uncatchable moods. When I approached from the side, preparatory to taking hold of his mane and slipping the bridle over his head and the bit into his mouth, he would swing away abruptly, showing me a clean pair of heels. Ever thought about that last phrase? I was in no mood to philosophise – I was tired and hungry and still had to ride up to the railway station for the newspapers and down to Downes's for the mail. If I digress to the Downeses and what that fine octogenarian, Ted Pound, told me about my grandfather's association with them I'll never get back to Glen Valley. I hope to remember to tell you later. It was about twenty years ago in Vin Marlo's pub at North Essendon.

Back to Boots. I decided to use shock tactics. I'd creep up on him from behind, slip along his near side, grab him by the mane and have him bridled before he knew what was happening. I miscalculated. The old bugger had read my mind. Just at the psychological moment (I'll tell you about that phrase, too, when I get a chance), he lashed out with both hind legs and landed me flat on my back in a pool of water. I found that night bruise marks on my left arm and chest. I didn't mention it at home. I don't think I've ever spoken of it since. We keep quiet about our mistakes. Anyhow Boots was satisfied to have made his point. I never again had trouble catching him.

It's true that other people still had trouble when they wanted to saddle up Boots. Once I saw him jump a fence with that chain on his leg, just to escape being caught. I don't know what his objection was on that occasion; perhaps he was a natural rebel. He wasn't much over fourteen hands and perhaps he would have been in the right in protesting if my father, six foot four and over thirteen stone, wanted to ride him. Dad on boots certainly would have looked better than Malcolm Fraser on a pony in one of his press release photographs. Dad could ride, with hands held low. Malcolm Fraser rides a horse as if it were a motorbike. Anyhow, I don't remember my father riding Boots, not even in the St Patrick's Day procession in St Arnaud. How proud I was of him in his magnificent green Hibernian sash; Dad I mean, not Boots.

Sutherland, Gooroc, Swanwater, Darkbonnie, Coonooer West, to the north and north-west of St Arnaud, combined to form an enclave of first generation Irish-Australians, rather like the district 'John O'Brien' wrote of in 'Around the Boree Log', and indeed the German-Australian district at Coromby, near Murtoa I was to know some years later. The school at Sutherland was, in effect, a Catholic school. Most of the forty or fifty pupils were of Irish descent and the teacher herself was a member of a well-known Swanwater family. The sons and daughters of two of her brothers attended. I think now that she must have been embarrassed when one Walsh family during the First World War ignored daylight saving and arrived each morning at ten fifteen. Classes began at 9.15. I shall have more to say, I hope, about Miss C Walsh in these chronicles. She was a dedicated teacher and I respected her. It was, however, something of a welcome relief when a rather good-looking teacher, much younger, took her place for a few months. Miss W. was ill. Legend had it that the only reason she wasn't a nun was that her health ruled her out.

Miss Herbert must have found the job of teaching eight grades a very difficult one. Some twelve years later, I did, and I had the advantage of a year at Melbourne Teachers College. She seemed to cope very well. I think she was there in 1916 or 1917. I say this for two reasons. My life-long friend's name was and is Paddy Hoye. He didn't like being called Pat. So I hug with delight the memory of that day when, after a session of multiplication tables at the blackboard and some oral testing, we were making our way back to our six-seating desks, I heard dear, lovely Miss Herbert call 'Pat, Pat, come back here, Pat'.

Miss Herbert decided to celebrate Empire Day by inviting all the parents to spend the afternoon at the school, taking a passive part in a demonstration, in song and recitation of the district's loyalty to Throne and Empire. When the bell rang for the afternoon assembly, the charming, comely Miss H must have felt rather deflated. The only parent who attended was our Mum.

This is not to say that the Irish-Catholic farmers of the area were more than sentimental supporters of the heroes of the Easter Rising. The 'Sixteen Dead Men' of W.B. Yeats had still not been executed. A Terrible Beauty had still not been born. There was a big St Patrick's Day march and sports in St Arnaud. I remember winning a race and receiving four shillings. But it wasn't enough to erase the memory of a miserable defeat in the 'pillow fight'. In case you haven't come across this particular form of athletic contest, I'll try to describe it. Take two boys, two sugar bags half-filled with sawdust, put them on a rail facing one another, say 'Go' and the one still sitting on the rail is the winner. In this contest Jack Seccombe was the winner. Jack was a town boy and I faced him with confidence. We all knew that country lads were better than town lads.

Furthermore, we had practised for this pillow fight on the cow-yard rails. I had several brothers and the ones who practised with me were probably Jack, Vincent and Ted. Jim, the eldest, would have thought it beneath his dignity and Frank, Kevin and Bernie were too young.

When I mounted the rail to face Jack S, I noticed that it was a piece of green timber, stripped of its bark. It was round and very slippery, not like our cow-yard fence at all. However, I was quite confident until the starter said 'Go' and Jack S. hit me and I hit the ground. I don't remember that Vin or Ted did any better, though both later showed considerable athletic ability. Jack, as the horseman of the family, could have retrieved our reputation. Jim, Jack, Frank, Kevin and Bernie are all dead: what am I doing here?

I started by telling you of my indecision as to which of two horses I would put my two bob on in the 1951 Caulfield Cup. This was at Glen Valley or Glen Wills. How I came to be living there for eighteen months is a much more interesting story. I'm saving it. Back now to Glen Valley and Glen Wills and my little betting problem.

I mentioned that I had been born at Kooreh, some six miles south of St Arnaud. The railway station was at Carapooee a couple of miles from our farm. A few years ago I read with regret that the railway station was closed. In the thirties I had two verses published in the Sydney Bulletin; 'Wheat' and 'Forty miles to Stawell'. In 1940 or '41, I wrote a 'war pome' for the Bulletin. I called it 'Stuttering Steve'. It was about a young Wimmera farmer or farmworker who became tired of driving a tractor and of his stammering mate, Steve. Yes, you've guessed it. In Egypt the inevitable happened. In 'Answers to Correspondents' I got 'Don't think Steve's very funny'. I thought Steve was funny and resented any criticism of my brain-child. Like Andy's in Lawson's 'The Loaded Dog', my mind began to work and I sent 'Steve' to Smith's Weekly. Smith's featured it on their back page, dedicated to the Australian soldier, illustrations and all. That was the beginning of a love affair, lasting some months, between Smith's and me. For further reference, see Chapter 8 'Bloody Blamey'.

During 1941, I forwarded a verse 'Carapooee Creek' to the Bulletin and received the comment 'Creek nearly trickled in'. This time I knew what to do. I changed the last stanza to suit Smith's soldiers' page. They published it. To give you a fair idea of my poetic qualifications as they then were, here is 'Carapooee Creek':

> I wonder does that creek, the Carapooee Creek,
> Still stubbornly adventure down the Kooreh hill;
> I wonder does it yet, attenuated , weak,
> Slip slenderly past boulders with the same old skill.
>
> The magpie's call at morn, a wattle-scented morn,
> Ringing down the valley, rippling, fading, then
> Expanding like emotion, a thought new-born,
> Could I hear it now, I wonder, hear that again?
>
> The blackfish in the pool, a slim bright streak,
> Gleaming like a bubble on a sparkling wine,
> Would it nibble shyly yet in Carapooee Creek
> At a boy's bait trembling on a home-made line?
>
> Perhaps if I went, a young boy again,
> I would see the rabbits running, dot, dash, dot,
> I would hear them thumping as I heard them when
> I held my shanghai ready for a swift, sure shot.
>
> I'd crawl to the sergeant, be sycophantic, meek,
> Just to get away from Egypt to see if still,
> That hesitating creek, the Carapooee Creek,
> Obstinately trickles down the Kooreh hill.

You're lucky. I remember in full only four of my published verses. As to the rest, ask the A.B.C.

Perhaps now you can see my difficulty in deciding which of the two horses, Grey Boots, the favourite, or Carapooee, an outsider. In the event, I put my two bob on the outsider which got nowhere. The favourite won. And I had drawn Carapooee in the pub sweep on the Saturday afternoon. Is there a place of that name in Queensland?

As an aside I'd like to tell you that I did get another twelve bob from 'Carapooee Creek'. I had always resented the fact that the Editor, who paid a few shillings for published verse claimed copyright in perpetuity. The most that I received from the Bulletin was twenty-four shillings for 'Forty Miles to Stawell'. Some other time, I'd like to tell you about the two guineas I got from Truth for a satirical verse about Stanley Bruce. Boxed on the front page it was. The good old Bulletin, in the late forties, gave me only twelve shillings for the original 'Creek'; I had changed only the name; to 'Kooreh Creek'. I was, for a time, indignant that the second stanza was omitted and part of it included in the last stanza. When I discovered that the poetry editor was Douglas Stewart, I thought ah well, he should know. The verse was the original 'Carapooee Creek'.

Some of my most pleasant memories are concerned with animals. There was that summer evening when I was riding a bicycle from Bright to Freeburgh. About a mile from Freeburgh, just before Tony Jack's place, I saw two men engaged in earnest conversation by the roadside. As I drew nearer, I called out cheerfully 'Good evening'. The result of this friendly greeting even frightened my bike; one fellow hopped, in great bounds, across the road in front of me, the other rapidly headed down towards the Ovens River. Yes, kangaroos. The only ones I had come across in some thirty years of life in the Victorian countryside.

I have never seen an emu. I missed a chance of seeing three of them, etched black against the mountain snow at Glen Wills, some thirty years ago. My younger son and daughter saw them up near Sunnyside when I took them for a walk. Where was I? In the pub. My son has been three times around the world since then but he still regards it as one of his most memorable experiences. With his wife and three children he was spending, this, his sabbatical year, in France. I have never been outside Victoria, the Kings St Bridge backwater, but my elder daughter and younger son have made up for it. My three granddaughters were born overseas, two in London, U.K. and one in Nashville, U.S.A. All my grand-children, including two grandsons, are living abroad this year, 1980.

I mentioned that I have never seen an emu but I have seen many wedge-tailed eagles; only two of them on the ground. That was at Freeburgh, in the Ovens Valley, when under the pine trees near the hall, they were trying to wrest a rabbit from my lovely little whipple-kelpie cross bitch, Nip. Nip finally became tired of their attentions and put them to flight. It was just as well for her that she was not out in the open. The heavily feathered legs of these birds did not quite register with me for many years. Not until, some thirty years later, I was told of the perceptive remark by little Cathie B, born within the sound of the Bow Bells. Cathie, at the age of four, was taken with her brothers and sisters to the Healesville Sanctuary. Sighting two eagles, wedge-tails, Cathie cried excitedly 'look Mum, them birds has got trousers on'. Cathie might yet be a poet. Do any readers remember that line about the robin: 'That little hunchback in the snow'? Cathies's remark seems to me to indicate a similar quality of acute perception.

I quote the line from Robert Lynd's magnificent essay, 'On poetry and the Modern Man' in that splendid anthology, 'Modern Verse' chosen by A. Methuen and first published in 1921. My tattered old copy shows that in 1926 it had reached its 21st edition. Thank you, Mr Fred Whelpton, of Melbourne Teachers College, 1928. I'll have more to say about poetry and teaching of poetry in another chapter. Cheer up; there's more to come.

Some years before this, I was at Lubeck, a small township in the Wimmera between Stawell and Horsham. Perhaps its only claim to fame is that my daughter Jennifer was born there. Now a Ph.D. (Lond) and a lecturer in English in that great metropolis, she is recognised as an authority on the English poets of the first World War, notably Wilfred Owen, one of the first to write of war as a filthy, dirty, murderous business.

At Lubeck, we used to get the Melbourne 'Herald' only on Saturdays. The bundle was thrown from the guard's van of the Adelaide express as it passed through at about midnight. By arrangement with the local storekeeper, I used to get my Herald from the bundle after the express went through. To reach the railway station, I had to cross the local park. The township had no public lighting and I knew the walk so well that I didn't bother to carry a torch. On this particular Saturday night I bumped into a solid, living, breathing obstruction. I said 'sorry' but there was no reply. 'Bad mannered b.' I muttered and struck a match. I found myself looking at the wrong end of a horse.

My first country school, as a teacher, a Head Teacher indeed, was at Arawata, a dairy farming district near Korumburra in South

Gippsland. Most of my memories are pleasant. I mention now one exception. Quite a number of the children rode ponies to school and, during my first week there, I was out watching them saddle up after school when I decided to saddle up six-year old Jimmie N's white pony. All went smoothly until I bent my head to study the marks on the girth as I tightened it. The pony suddenly showed its resentment of my ministration by turning its head and taking quite a sizeable hank of my hair between its teeth. That really hurt and I lost some hair but did not do my block. Though the children seemed suitably horrified, I became aware later that some parents were amused at a townie's lack of experience. And, dammit, I had been used to saddling up horses since I was Jimmie's age.

I wasn't much older than Jimmie when at Sutherlands school, near St Arnaud, I came out after all the others had gone and found my Shetland pony, Sailor, bridled and saddled, waiting for me. I don't know why I was late out because I certainly wasn't kept in for misbehaviour or failure to learn. Miss Walsh regarded me, because of my very good memory and lack of trouble in learning to read, as her prize pupil. More of that another time.

Anyhow, I accepted the saddling of Sailor as a friendly gesture from my friend Paddy. Now, sixty-five or more years later, I am still inclined to believe in the essential goodness of human nature. I should be living in the U.S.S.R., or, at least, some socialist country. Without incident, I rode the Shetland the half-mile to the railway station to pick up the AGE, the WEEKLY TIMES or the LEADER. Then I headed down to pick up the mail from Mrs Downes. Mrs D. was one of the family that had been friends of my grandfather back to 1870. Tell you about that another time. I wasn't more than a furlong, two hundred metres, from the station when I suddenly found myself flat on the back with my saddle on top of me. Yes, Paddy had left the point of the buckle out of the hole in the girth. Was it fun or was it envy? Envy of what?

Some ten years later...

Chapter 3 – A pig of a man

As a youngster in a rural school of some forty-odd pupils in a wheat-farming district north of St Arnaud in Victoria I have pleasant memories. This particular school was attended by boys and girls who were mostly Catholics, not so much Roman Catholics as Irish-Australian Catholics. As a very young man, I thought that all bigots were Protestants, notably Orangemen and Freemasons. I still regard the Orangemen as bigoted but certainly no more so than Frank McManus and his Democratic Labor Party, D.L.P. which was always, in effect, the Decoy Liberal Party. The bigotry of bishops, priests and, in Victoria, about one-third of the laity, really shocked me, and I cut my last links with the Church. I shall refer to my lost faith in another Chapter.

The D.L.P. whose candidates always gave their second preferences to the Liberal Party which, in Australia is composed almost entirely of conservatives and re-actionaries, exercised a quite disproportionate effect on State and Federal politics. So much so that when the U.S.A. President, L.B. Johnson, wanted to withdraw from the dreadful slaughter, and the Australian Prime Minister, John Gorton, also wanted out, they were frustrated by the Australian D.L.P. and the Australian National Civic Council, led by B.A. Santamaria ('Arriba Espana, Viva

Franco'). Santamaria was the real deus ex machina in Catholic political intervention, Frank McManus was just his puppet. Yes, I know Frank. I was with him on the first Catholic Young Men's Society Debating Board in 1928. We succeeded Mick Chamberlin, later Sir Michael and Chancellor of Monash University. As I, a spondylitic* septuagenarian, see my life drawing to a close, I am glad that, unlike Frank and 'Bob', I do not have the death and dismemberment of hundreds of thousands of Vietnamese and Kampucheans on my conscience.

The Head Teacher, the only teacher, at the Sutherland school was Miss Walsh; she was a daughter of one of the early settlers. Her nephews and nieces, of the Mick Walsh and Pat Walsh families, attended the school. They were good people, like all the other families in the Suthereland-Swanwater-Gooroc-Darkbonnie district but perhaps she found their attendance embarrassing. As at the time of daylight saving in the First World War when the Pat Walsh boys arrived at school at a quarter past ten instead of nine-fifteen. I like the story of Joe W. at a wake told to me by my brother Frank who kept in touch with St Arnaud largely because he married a girl from Coonooer West. That's east of Gooroc, beyond the Black Stump. I spent my best holiday ever at Coonooer West when I was eighteen. I hope to tell that story later. Anyhow, Frank is now dead as are five of my brothers.

I still don't quite understand why Miss Walsh, a competent and dedicated teacher, had a few older pupils sitting round a table in this somewhat overcrowded one-room school. After all there were two perfectly good secondary schools just six miles away. The St Arnaud High School and the St Arnaud Convent run by those very good in-

---

* See footnote 2.

structors, the Sisters of Mercy. It did me indirectly some good; I had to copy out, at Miss W's suggestion, the whole of the Commentaries of Caesar for my eldest brother, Jim. I don't think that Miss W's post-primary ventures lasted more than a year or two. Perhaps the School Inspector put his foot down and so he should have. My only other criticism of Miss Walsh is that she promoted me from the sixth grade to the eighth. This affected me all through my secondary education.

I have much to say in praise of Miss Walsh and I will. I want to now speak of the real significance of my chapter heading. Do you yet detect the influence of Caesar's Commentaries? I was used to big men as a boy. My father was six foot four and about thirteen stone. There were others like him thereabouts. I see now that my impression of a big man revealed a kindly, tolerant gentleman but there was one big fellow that I met twice a year whom I didn't like at all. This was a Mr Lowry, the School Inspector. He obviously terrorised both teachers and pupils. A gruff, ill-mannered standover merchant, he would have been quite unable to see the children in a rural school, any school, as they really were. They would have been too nervous to show what they could do in either written or oral tests. I have sometimes speculated since that he might have been an Orangeman and didn't like the preponderance of Irish names on the school roll. But I take my chapter heading from the remark made by Mr Thos. G. Strange, the Englishman from Yorkshire or somewhere close to the Scottish border, who was Head Teacher at Glenroy State School where I was a Junior Teacher for more than three years. Once in a conversation with Mr. Strange I mentioned Inspector Lowry. He snorted, saying 'He was a pig of a man'.

I still remember how pleased we all were at the Sutherland school when Mr. Gill replaced Mr. Lowry as District Inspector. I was probably eleven years old then and was occasionally kept home to help about the house or assist my father with some job in the paddocks. On this particular day, we were walking through the sheep in a paddock near the road that led to the school and the railway station; it was lambing time and we were there to assist ewes in trouble, a rather unpleasant job I found it. A well-dressed man went riding by on his bicycle, a bag (portmanteau?) on the handle. My father knew it had to be the School Inspector; only twice a year did we see a man, always well-dressed, on a bike. The policeman who came once a year to collect information for some census always rode a horse. And very impressive he appeared in his Mounted Police uniform. I still get a giggle from the story about my good friend, Paddy H. The whole family was having lunch – we call it dinner there – Mr. & Mrs. H., ten-year old Paddy and his five sisters, the 'girl', or young woman who helped in the house, and the 'man' who helped outdoors when a knock came at the door. 'Come in if your fat, stay out if your thin'. When a policeman entered, Paddy was so embarrassed that he disappeared under the table. However, my source for this may be as unreliable as those of our newspapers that continue to tell ridiculous stories about Russia and the magnificent success of its gigantic experiments. I write in 1980, just before the Olympic Games in Moscow. I'll need at least a chapter to outline the events leading up to these Games; it will probably be headed 'The Busted Boycott'.

Back to the new School Inspector. My father immediately sent me home to get changed for school. My mother probably wrote a note for me to explain my very late arrival. I forget whether I walked the mile and a bit that day or rode a pony but, as Mr Lowry was the only Inspector I had met, I could not have been looking forward to meeting his successor.

I was in for a pleasant surprise. The comparatively young Mr Gill – I estimate now that he was in his mid-forties – seemed to have as his chief object, not finding fault with the teacher and the pupils, but in introducing them to new horizons, to a better and more exciting world. With hindsight, I think that he persuaded Miss Walsh to have the boys and girls playing together, at least under supervision. Otherwise how was it we found ourselves joining the girls in a rounders match? And in school time? I, for one, was really enjoying this new experience when God came to the aid of Miss Walsh and the other Puritans in the local community. Have you ever noticed that the Irish-Australian Catholic is much more conservative, sexually, than the Methodist or Presbyterian? They'll give the grog an open go; do they regard it as a suitable substitute for sex?

Back to the rounders. I hope you don't want me to explain how a lively, nine-year old, boy can break his leg playing rounders. I have, through a life-time experience of schools and school grounds, seen quite a variety of accidents but never since Billy Allen managed it have I known a leg broken in a game of rounders. No, Billy hadn't an Irish name nor did any of the several families who occupied the railway residences provided for the fettlers and their families. I understand that Patsy Adam Smith, a splendid Australian writer, came from such a family. I am not surprised. I fancy it was good for us to learn that Protestants, though they might be doomed to the eternal torments of Hell, were such really pleasant people. Anyhow the likeable Billy's accident put an end to a game period at Sutherland State School. Such a clear sign from Heaven could not be ignored.

I fancy, too, that Mr Gill indicated to Miss W. that the reading by the teacher to the middle and senior grades of such poems as Longfellow's 'Hiawatha' and Matthew Arnold's 'Sohrab and Rustum' was a step in the right direction. I may be unfair to Miss W. in this. I do remember that my elder sister and I used to look forward each year to another Billabong book by Mary Grant Bruce and these we must have obtained from the school library, long before Mr. Gill's coming. I think now that Miss Walsh was a really dedicated teacher. A few weeks after we came to Rye, this normally pleasant seaside township, to live in retirement, we received, with our milk delivery, an appeal from the Mother's Club at the Rye State Primary School, for a donation to buy books for the school library. This, according to the writer, was 'almost non-existent'. I was shocked to find that in 1973, in a prosperous town, such a state of affairs should exist. I sent two dollars and a letter congratulating all those concerned with the appeal but deploring the lack of effort in the past on the part of the local School Committee. I shall quote from this letter in the chapter headed 'Intransigence'. Queer things began to happen.

Now I come to the second 'Pig of a Man' I had the misfortune to meet. This was at Ocean Grove where, in the late thirties, I was the Head Teacher of the local State Primary School. Yes, this one, too, was a School Inspector. He, too, was a big man physically. I was to find that, in other respects, he was a mean, little creature. My first School Inspector at Ocean Grove was a Mr. Ashton who had started me off at my first rural school at Arawata near Korumburra a few years before on a Very Good teaching mark. This put me in the first sub-division of Class V, big deal. He was also a big man, not only physically. My father would have called him a gentleman. But Mr. J .G. Cannon was no gentleman. He frightened Hell out of the forty-odd youngsters at Ocean Grove. I still do not understand his hostile attitude on a first visit just a few days before the end of the school year, my second at Ocean Grove. The school was in a rather better condition, in all respects, than it had been. All my eighth grade pupils, in both years, had passed their Merit Certification examinations. Mr. Cannon's predecessor, Mr. Ashton, had been pleased with my effort. It was he indeed who had given me my first Very Good mark at Arawata in 1929.

I have pondered much, in my retirement years, on the reasons for Cannon's initial antagonism and now think it likely that Eric Spriggins, then Head Teacher of a fourth-class neighbouring school, may have been responsible. I found him, some twenty years later, as a mean-minded, gossipy, old woman. I had first known Eric in 1928 when a student at Melbourne Teachers' College. He was then a class teacher at one of the inner suburban schools where we spent a morning or two a week as part of our training. It is only now, in retrospect, that I see that Eric was really hurt when, in 1939, at a meeting in Leopold I was elected President of the local State Schools' Sports Association. I believe now that he had expected to replace Fred Dyson, the Leopold H.T., as President. His disappointment might well have made him make derogatory remarks to Cannon regarding myself. I can find no other reason, except this speculation.

At the time I considered it very likely that Cannon's antagonism resulted from my leader-page article in the Melbourne 'Herald' concerning the Merit Certificate examination and the general lack of secondary education opportunities. I called it 'Musings on the Merit' by 'Chaos'. In the article I had tried to conceal my identity. I'd already had verses published by the 'Bulletin' and the 'Australasian', considered then as Australia's best literary magazines and when I sent to the 'Herald' my criticism of the Merit Certificate examination and the general attitude of teachers and inspectors to the right of children to secondary education, I wrote 'Here's something good for your Saturday Literary Magazine'. This was in December, 1936.

At this time, by arrangement with the local store-keeper at Lubeck, I used to walk across to the railway station and take my Saturday 'Herald' from the bundle thrown at midnight from the Adelaide express. But nowhere in the literary pages could I find my brain-child. 'The stupid bastards' I thought and proceeded to read the newspaper, starting at the front page. On the Editorial page I was delighted to find 'Musings on the Merit' by 'Chaos'*. I had, I thought, quite cleverly concealed my identity and could probably, almost certainly, have got away with it if I'd kept my mouth shut but my pleasure in being promoted to the leader-page induced me to show it to two or three locals. In a life studded with mistakes this was a serious one. Who am I to say Gough Whitlam lacked judgement?

I had already learned that the local school inspector, Norman McHutchison, had a local contact, a farmer. Jim Hall, who worked for this farmer, had told me that McHutchison had said of me, referring to a speech that I made at the Murtoa Hibernian Communion Breakfast, reported in full in the 'Dunmunkle Standard', 'He's talking against

* See https://trove.nla.gov.au/newspaper/article/244657191?browse=nd-p%3Abrowse%2Ftitle%2FH%2Ftitle%2F1190%2F1936%2F12%2F05%2F-page%2F26604585%2Farticle%2F244657191

his bread-n-butter'. I see now that in this small matter, Mac was right. Anyhow, this inspector had, like Mr. Ashton at Arawata, strongly recommended that I should qualify academically to become an inspector.

So, after Mr Cannon's first visit to Ocean Grove, I came to the conclusion that his hostility was due to his awareness of my authorship of 'Musings on the Merit', my Herald article. I had, over the past few years, had two verses published in the Victorian Teachers' Journal, a Teachers' Union publication. Now I sent my first attempt at free verse to the V.T.U. Secretary, Mr Fred Thomas, M.A. He had published my two previous satirical efforts in his own column. I remember only the first stanza and scraps of others. I do not recall any line in the last stanza. A remark made by Inspector J. Davidson to me in front of Assistant Chief Inspector Leach at Freeburgh a few months after I left Ocean Grove puzzled me for year. In fact, it was only since I retired that I found the answer. More of that later. I'm in a hurry now. Certain things must be written down. Back to my 'modern poem':

> I do not know of anyone under the sun
> Who suffers more
> From inspectors
> Than I do;
> When they call, full of self-importance
> And often not much else
> Except a hearty breakfast
> Which fifth-class teachers cannot afford
> I get the jitters somewhat.

It was a light-hearted effort and I remember only scraps of the next two stanzas –

'Of poetry such as mine
And writes 'Poetry is not well-known'.

Mr. Thomas returned the verse with the explanation that the Editorial Committee had declined to publish it and, in any case, he himself preferred verse in the traditional form. But of course, there were teachers on the Editorial Committee who licked their chops and rubbed their hands with glee! 'He's having a go at Cannon!' It took me nearly forty years to arrive at this conclusion. Don't talk to me about Malcolm Fraser being a slow developer.

Mr Cannon's first visit to the Ocean Grove school occurred just a few days before the December break-up. I shall deal with it in some detail later. I was surprised at his hostility and assumed that he was aware of the identity of 'Chaos' writer of the 'Herald' article 'Musings on the Merit'. However, on his second visit, in the first six months of 1940, his hostility was even more obvious. Indeed it seemed to have become a personal matter with him and I responded in a similar fashion. See the chapter 'Intransigence'.

I applied later that year for the position of Head Teacher at Freeburgh, near Bright in the Ovens Valley, chiefly because I wanted a school residence. The housing situation at Ocean Grove was unsatisfactory. I got the appointment but the H.T. at Freeburgh asked me, because his wife was in hospital, to delay transferring my family and furniture so we went to my parent's home at Essendon. Early in January of 1941 I was in the public bar at Young and Jackson's Hotel in Melbourne, holding my ten oz handle pot in my hand, when two well-dressed men approached the bar from the other side. They each ordered and were given a glass of beer and were continuing their earnest conversation, which seemed to be dominated by the bigger man, when he suddenly caught my eye. I waved my pot cheerily trying to express in one simple friendly gesture my contempt for him and all his kind and my pleasure in leaving forever the sphere of his influence. He put down his glass untasted, said a word or two to his companion and they both vanished, disappeared; they weren't there anymore. Yes, a few months later, I discovered that his companion was my new inspector, Mr. J. D. Davidson.

Yes, Jimmy whom I learned to know with affectionate contempt was Cannon's friend at Young & Jackson's when they evanesced at the sight of me. I thought that I'd lost Cannon but I had acquired a very weak imitation of a 'Pig of a Man'. He didn't act up to it successfully. On his first 'incidental' visit in the first half-year, he was far from enthusiastic about my school, at all, at all. Later in the year he was accompanied by an Assistant Chief Inspector, a mean-minded little man who must surely have been responsible for the production of the Merit Certificate papers which I had lashed quite severely just three or four years before in the Melbourne 'Herald'. He was even less enthusiastic than Jimmy. He appeared to have a personal grudge against me.

I must mention here before retiring from writing memoirs. During the visit at Freeburgh of the two inspectors, a remark from Jimmy puzzled me for many years. He said to me 'Didn't you make a pun about Mr Cannon?' I replied to the effect that I had never spoken to anybody about Cannon (I nearly said 'the big gun') but I expressed the opinion that the pun was the lowest form of wit. I noticed during this earnest, little conversation that assistant chief inspector Leech nudged him with his elbow. Why did Leech nudge Jimmy when he asked about Cannon's pun? I gave up.

That was a mistake, another one of mine. It wasn't until I retired that I realised that Cannon had known of my light-hearted satirical verse about inspectors, notably my piggish mate. Somebody had taken a copy of my criticism and had showed it to his friends. 'Of course he means Cannon; he's down at Ocean Grove, in his inspectorate'. **[NB: This was as far as the autobiography got to.]**

Acknowledgments

I wish to acknowledge and thank a number of people who assisted me in the preparation of this memoir. My younger sister, Sue Munday, triggered some additional memories and gave me permission to write about our family. Sadly, my older brother, Michael, and my older sister, Jennifer, are both deceased but I think that they too would be happy to see the lives of our parents honoured in this way.

Anne Black, on behalf of the extended Black family, approved my writing about Anne's parents, Patricia and Adrian Black.

Pauline McCall and Diann Talbot, volunteers at the Bright and District Historical Society Museum, generously spent time seeking images of the Freeburgh area and its gold dredge. They also drew my attention to some valuable books that have been written about Bright and the region.

Nick Walker and his wonderful team at Australian Scholarly Publishing yet again have been very helpful and have produced a very attractive design for the book.

www.ingramcontent.com/pod-product-compliance
Ingram Content Group Australia Pty Ltd
76 Discovery Rd, Dandenong South VIC 3175, AU
AUHW020841060325
407965AU00004B/56

9 781923 068957